Pure Joy!

The Positive Side of Single Sexuality

RICK STEDMAN

MOODY PRESS
CHICAGO

*To Amy, my "billion dollar table,"
who continues to teach me what
it means to truly value someone.*

CONTENTS

Preface   9

Part 1:
Why Did God Make Me This Way?

1. Can Singles Thank God for Sexuality?   19
2. How Much Are Singles Worth Sexually?   27
3. Why Do Singles Sometimes Feel Worthless?   39
4. God's Surprising Answer: The Value of Single Sexuality   53

Part 2:
Why Does God Leave My Sex Switches On?

5. Does Sex Guarantee Intimacy?   69
6. Why Did God Make Us Male and Female?   81
7. What Is the Hidden Purpose Behind Single Sexuality?   95
8. How Can I Handle Temptation?   107

Part 3:
How Far Is Too Far?

9. Should Sexual Intimacy Increase with Commitment?   121
10. Should Singles Feel Compelled to Be Sexually Intimate?   135
11. How Full Is Your Moral Bank Account?   145
12. What About Living Together Before Marriage?   157

Part 4:
Tough Questions and Value-Filled Answers

13. Intimacy, Gender, and Commitments   171
14. Incompatibility, Attractiveness, and Single Parenting   183
15. Masturbation, Fantasies, and Lust   195

Notes   209

PREFACE

I came from one of those backgrounds where nothing sexual was ever explained clearly," Jeff told me, "but somehow or another I was supposed to know what was right and what was wrong. Even as a devoted Christian, I didn't always do what was right in God's eyes because I had nothing but don'ts to go on. I wish this positive message could have reached my ears twenty-five years earlier."

Jeff is not alone. Most single adults want a positive approach to their sexuality. They need it in order to understand themselves better and to be able to make healthy decisions regarding their sexual behavior. They hear the "Thou shalt nots" and wonder why. But others need a positive, biblical approach to single sexuality too. Children and teens need it in order to feel positively about their sexuality and have a positive reason to limit their sexual activity. Parents of children and teens need it in order to know how to talk to their kids about sex and how to set appropriate boundaries. Church pastors, leaders, and teachers need it to be able to understand why God gave the guidelines He did in the Bible, so they will be able to say more than just, "Don't do it because God says so." Married people need it in order to understand the struggles their single friends face and to be be able to support them better.

Whatever your station in life—whether church leader or layperson, adult or teen, believer or doubter, single or married—sexuality is a gift from God intended by Him to protect and assert your deep value. That is the heart of this message. That truth should be embraced by singles, who often find their status one in which they (or those they know) conclude they are worth less than married adults and devalued physically. And for the majority of Christian single adults who have heard only "Don't" for many years, this biblical perspective will help bring the resolution and strength for a commitment to celibacy that many have longed for.

WHERE WE'RE GOING

Pure Joy! is designed to help the millions of singles who, like Jeff, need more than don'ts—they need a positive approach to single sexuality.

The book is divided into four parts: Part one presents the positive side of single sexuality; part two deals with the reason God keeps our sexual switches on; part three answers that bottom-line question, "How far is too far?" and presents a completely new ethical guideline for single sexual behaviors; part four gives answers to the really tough questions that singles ask about such topics as fantasies, lust, masturbation, and sexual incompatibility.

Together, they offer a completely new approach to the theology of sexuality and its application to single sexuality. At the end of each chapter are discussion questions designed to help singles talk through these important issues.

By the very nature of the subject, *Pure Joy!* will deal with issues, events, words, and even bodily parts and functions that don't usually find their way into genteel speech and Christian conversations. So a caution: Fasten your seatbelt—there are curves ahead. For a time I considered censoring some quotes and statements, not wanting to offend anyone. But I quickly realized that to do so would be a disservice to the many singles who desperately need an honest, straightforward discussion of single sexuality. Each chapter contains statements by singles (called "A Single Speaks") that at times may surprise you. Since every single—even a Christian single—has a sexual history, I asked singles in several different churches and colleges to write down the story of their own sexuality for possible use in this book. Frankly, knowing how difficult it is to be honest with someone else about such matters (it's even difficult to be honest with ourselves!), I didn't expect to get very complete or vulnerable responses. Was I ever surprised! As I read page after page of heart-wrenching accounts, I found myself deeply moved.

I have chosen to include several of these accounts and not censor them too much, so that the singles struggling with such past experiences can discover they are not alone. As one single woman said after reading a rough draft of this manuscript, "It's so good to know that I'm not the only one who has been hurt sexually and who struggles in this area. Because of my terrible childhood and some mistakes I made as an adult, I thought there was something wrong with me, and I've kept all these thoughts hidden inside me for my whole Christian life. But as I read some of the testimonies from singles in your book, I was amazed that they too have had it rough. That alone was a healing experience for me!"

Not every single person has such sexual experiences, of course. By God's grace, some have remained chaste, resisting temptation. However, reading these accounts will remind you of the struggles that all singles face, both virgins and non-virgins. As one married women told me after reading a draft of the book, "Wow. I've lived a sheltered life! I had no idea singles struggled with such deep things. I have more respect now for my single friends!"

WATCH OUT—IT'S EASY TO JUDGE

In fact, let's be honest here—no one's past is perfectly pure in the sexual arena. Jesus made this clear in Matthew 5:27-30. He did not say, *"If anyone* looks on a woman lustfully," but instead, *"Everyone* that looks on a woman lustfully has already committed adultery with her in his heart" (NASB*; emphasis added). I think Jesus knew that sexuality is a problem that all of us face; He knew that no one would be perfect in this area (except Himself).

Is there really anyone who has never allowed a sexually tempting situation or visual stimulation to produce lustful thoughts? I think not. President Jimmy Carter, in his famous interview with *Playboy* magazine, spoke for "Everyman" when he admitted to having lusted on occasion. I believe Jesus was pointing out that all of us are sinners in many common areas. We all have been angry with someone and thus have sinned emotionally. We all have desired revenge and hated enemies and thus have sinned socially. We all have broken oaths and promises and thus have sinned mentally. We all have at least once in our lives given in to lustful thoughts and thus have sinned sexually. We are sinners in every area of human existence: emotional, social, mental, and physical.

As Paul said, "All have sinned and fall short of the glory of God" (Romans 3:23). Specifically, we each need to come to the realization

* New American Standard Bible.

that in addition to the other areas, that verse means that we all have sinned sexually and have fallen short of God's glory.

I would caution the reader to avoid casting judgments on these singles. Some of them have made big mistakes, but we all have. Fortunately, we have a Savior who generously forgives. But He doesn't forgive some more than others; it didn't take just half of His death on the cross to forgive some and the whole death to forgive the really bad ones. No, we each need the whole thing. As we kneel at the cross asking forgiveness, remember that we all kneel on level ground.

Because as humans we all are sexual people, I hope that every reader—single or married, virgin or not—will be able to see himself or herself on the pages of this book. Problems with sexuality are part and parcel of the human condition. After reading the "A Single Speaks" sections, Shannon wrote me a quick note. "Because of their stories, I decided that I needed to clean out that closet. I'm going to write my own sexual history and give it to you, because I want at least one other human being to know the truth about me. Then you can reassure me that I've been forgiven by God. I know you will keep it confidential— you had better keep it confidential! Maybe if you remind me that God has forgiven me, then I will be able to finally forgive myself and feel pure again."

WRITING YOUR SEXUAL AUTOBIOGRAPHY

Her words caused me to think, *How many singles and marrieds would also benefit from writing their own sexual autobiographies?* The obvious answer is: all of us! I encourage you at some point during the reading of this book to take out several sheets of paper and write out your own sexual autobiography. It is an exercise of great healing and value. Tell the whole story from childhood on, even those events you'd rather forget. Yes, it will be painful to write; it will be like taking a scalpel to your own soul. But as with all surgeries, the immediate pain is justified by the long-term benefits. In fact, I would go so far as to say that until you write your sexual autobiography, you will not deal completely with these issues in your life. Putting it on paper is a huge step. It's like what the management specialists tell us about goal-setting: if we haven't written our goals down, we haven't really set any goals.

I am deeply indebted to those brave singles (and former singles) who took the time to write out their sexual histories and shared those with me. I am also profoundly grateful to the hundreds of singles who have shared with me their personal and sexual struggles in confidential counseling sessions over the years. All of these singles were my teachers, and I had much to learn. I know that their honesty with me greatly helped in my understanding of the whole issue of sexuality, and, as a result, greatly improved the contents of this book.

Lest there be any misconceptions, let me add that I am not a therapist, though I have several counseling sessions per week; I mainly do crisis intervention and pastoral counseling. At heart I am a pastor and evangelist, and I believe strongly that true healing and wholeness can only come through a personal relationship with God through Jesus Christ. Why I believe that is another story, but it is important to grasp my perspective if you are to understand how I approach singles and their sexuality. I seldom will allow more than one or two sessions with a specific individual; I always refer to licensed Christian counselors those who need therapy. In almost each session, though, I tell the counselee, "It is an honor for me to have this hour with you. Thank you so much for trusting me with your story and friendship." And I mean that. It is a privilege to be taken into someone's confidence in such intimate and personal areas.

Through counseling sessions and the sexual autobiographies, I quickly learned that almost every person has not only a sexual history, but a *significant* sexual history. Even the few who started their letters with "Since I am a virgin, I don't have anything important or exciting to tell you about . . ." recounted intense struggles with their sex drives, loneliness, feelings of self-worth, and guilt. I guess it simply is impossible to live in this sexually supercharged society and not struggle with one's sexual identity.

Because you are a sexual person, you will probably be unable to read this book in a detached, analytical manner. You will be ushered into the lives of other people, exposed to their experiences and feelings. You will hear people talk about thoughts, feelings, and events that have happened to you. You will read accounts that will sound strangely like your own. You may even have repressed memories uncovered by the pathos or parallelism between these stories and your own history. If you read this book with openness and honesty, you will be changed.

A PERSONAL WORD

Writing this book has helped in my own pilgrimage, but it has also raised some nagging doubts: Should I really write it? What qualifies me to write it? What if some of my friends read it who know that I am not perfect in this (or any other) area? At first, I thought this book should be written by someone with a more spotless past than my own. But then I realized (actually, I learned this from singles) that there really is no one with a spotless past. All of us, except Jesus, have sinned and fallen short of God's glory physically and sexually.

With much fear and trembling, then, I have undertaken this project. If it is of help to you, then Paul's words will once again have been fulfilled, "[The Lord] said to me, 'My grace is sufficient for you, for my power is made perfect in weakness.' Therefore I will boast all the more gladly about my weaknesses, so that Christ's power may rest on me. . . . For when I am weak, then I am strong." (2 Corinthians 12:9–10)

I write this not out of perfection but poverty. When the newspapers revealed the account of yet another minister to fall sexually, a friend said to me, "It's a good thing, Rick, that you don't have any skeletons in your closet." I responded, "Since when is my closet empty? I've got skeletons in my closet, just like everyone else. The difference in my life is that my closet door is open. I haven't tried to hide my sins and pretend as if I were perfect." And in a strange way, that has made my ministry more powerful than had I tried to appear faultless and pristine. None of us are, and even church leaders should admit that. Fortunately, I have learned to forgive myself and others for those skeletons. I pray this book will enable you to do the same.

SPECIAL THANKS

This book is the fruit of ministry with single adults. Singles ministry is a strange beast. For most church workers, it is looked down upon and seen as an unimportant portion of God's kingdom. But for those of us in singles ministry, it is life and ministry at its very best. Singles are wonderful people whose lives may not have turned out as they had once planned. Given just a bit of love and encouragement, they blossom into some of the finest Christians and best church workers I have ever known. In a healthy singles ministry, true love, support, accountability, and community take place.

I have been privileged to be involved for ten years with singles who have been my students and teachers, counselees and counselors. Their insights fill the pages of this book. I hope they realize how deeply indebted I feel to them and how much I value their friendships. Thanks to all of you.

I also would like to thank some special people in my life: Julia Staton, who was an invaluable help to me in her numerous roles as ministry assistant, typist, editor, and friend. Joan Brown and the Crossroads Singles, who do the real work of ministry and who have strongly supported this project. The staff, leaders, and members of Crossroads Christian Church in Corona, who loved me back into the ministry when I was just about to throw in the towel. The editorial staff at Moody Press, who have treated me very well—like a $600 table! My parents, family, and friends, who have believed in, supported, and consistently encouraged me over the years. And finally to my wife Amy, to whom this book is dedicated. It was she, more than anyone or anything else, who taught me what it means to truly value someone.

PART ONE

WHY DID GOD MAKE ME THIS WAY?

CHAPTER ONE

CAN SINGLES THANK GOD FOR SEXUALITY?

During the Middle Ages, Christian couples were encouraged to abstain from sex on Thursday out of respect for the Lord's Supper (instituted by Jesus on Maundy Thursday), on Friday for the crucifixion, on Saturday to honor the Virgin Mary, on Sunday for the resurrection, and on Monday in memory of the poor departed souls (with whom by this time they felt very sympathetic). Their slogan, therefore, became "Thank God It's Tuesday."[1]

But for modern Christian single adults, Tuesday never comes. Even medieval marrieds were able to experience and enjoy their sexuality two days a week, but today's singles feel as if they are never given a chance to thank God for their sexuality. That is because the only instruction they have heard from Christian leaders is "Don't!" As a result, Christian single adults often feel that sexual behavior for single Christians is never appropriate. While singles are clearly told what not to do sexually, they are not told what to do on the positive side, and thus the chance to thank God for their sexuality never comes.

If you are a single adult, this stress on the negative has probably left you feeling frustrated and resentful about both sexuality and the church. The Bible may seem to you a "thou shalt not" list, church leaders a bunch of prudes, and the single life a prison sentence to solitary confinement. Being a single adult can seem more like a punishment than a blessing when all you ever hear is the negative.

As a single, you may conclude that thanking God for your sexuality is being a hypocrite; after all, you don't feel grateful as an unmarried person. But *you can thank God* for your sexuality. This book will show you how. It will help you turn a trial into a triumph. James 1:2 says, "Consider it pure joy . . . whenever you face trials of many kinds." At last, singles can find in their sexuality a source of pure joy!

If you are not single, this book may clarify a confusion about singles that you have had. It can give you a new focus, so that you can say, "Now I understand why singles struggle so much and why they feel so frustrated. I need to start treating my single friends differently, and learn a positive side so that I can stress the good rather than just the bad." No matter what your marital status, there is a positive side to single sexuality that is important to learn.

THE PROBLEM OF SEXUALITY

Sexuality is a major problem for single adults, but it seldom shows up very high on surveys of singles' needs (except anonymous surveys), because most singles are embarrassed to admit they have sexual desires and conflicts. Many cannot even admit this to themselves. Sexuality is a taboo subject, especially in Christian circles. Many parents are unwilling or unsure how to present sexuality to their children. They may simplify or try to downplay their child's sexual identity; even pastors may do this (read "A Single Speaks"). Yet all of us, as human beings, must deal with sexual feelings.

A SINGLE SPEAKS

In many ways, the history of my sexual development was typical. Unfortunately, it laid the foundation for the problems that occurred later in my life.

I was the oldest of four children, born into a minister's family. My father was very strict, and my mother was very supportive of my father. There was very little nurturing that I remember as a child. There certainly was no discussion of sex at all.

My sex education consisted of what I learned in health classes in school, in the locker room with the 'boys' . . . . I wish [my father] would have helped me to understand my sexuality, how to treat girls, how to deal with my feelings during adolescence. Even though I was a virgin on my wedding night as far as actual intercourse was concerned, I certainly was not a virgin, since I had experienced lots of fondling and oral sex.

From the time of late high school and all during college, I had many girl friends. Too many of the relationships resulted in what one might call heavy petting. There were many times when our hands certainly did not remain outside our clothes. . . . I see now that I really didn't respect myself or the girls I dated. Even the woman who became my wife was not treated with the respect she deserved. There were many times when we would bring each other to orgasm.

I think to a great extent I carried a lot of guilt and shame regarding sex and sexuality into marriage. As a result, my wife and I never discussed our sexuality. Our love-making became routine, and our marriage soon lacked the true intimacy that a healthy sexual relationship should have. My anger over being 'forced' to have a vasectomy and her unwillingness to have any more children, along with the need for intimacy, laid the foundation for the affairs that later occurred in my life. As a result, my wife and I have now been estranged for five years, and as I write, I am in the process of filling out divorce papers.

I am not saying that if I had a healthier attitude toward sex and my own sexuality that what happened wouldn't have happened, but I really do feel that I would not be experiencing the regrets I am today.

One thing I have done, partially I think to redeem myself if that is possible, is to develop a much more open relationship with my son. When he was twelve, he and I went on a weekend away and had a good discussion about his sexuality. In the intervening years, we have maintained a good relationship and have been able to share a great deal together. It is one very good spot in my life, and I hope in his.

I don't know if I will ever again be in a caring, sexual relationship. Part of me feels that I do not deserve to be, especially after what I have done. However, this recent class, your lecture, and some self discovery, has done a lot that has helped to begin a healing in my life. I hope and pray that some day God will grant me the experience of a truly joyful, positive, and God-pleasing sexual relationship."

The man's story in "A Single Speaks" is like that of thousands of singles, many of whom share his secret desire to be taught about sexuality in a positive, open way. Unfortunately, very few families and churches are comfortable talking and teaching about this subject. When was the last time you heard a sermon in church on single sexuality? If you are one of the few who have ever heard one, the main point probably was: sex for singles is wrong and is to be avoided at all costs. The usual refrain sounds something like this, "It won't be easy, but that's God's command for single adults."

To be fair, today's preachers and writers are not that blunt and insensitive to singles anymore. Some will not say *command* anymore, believing it sounds too authoritarian. Instead, the current terminology suggests that God has some *principles* for successful single living, some moral *guidelines* that, when followed, bring singles fulfillment and holiness. Yes, they still are commands and cannot be ignored, but they must be presented with compassion and positive reasons why. However, even when they are called *principles* and *guidelines* they are like glazed donuts for the person who must eat—underneath the sugar-glaze covering is the same old command. The coating just makes it a little easier to swallow.

According to such teaching, God's message to singles is a simple no, without any accompanying positive reasoning for it. As one single man put it, "I can tell you what the church's whole theology of single sexuality is in one simple word—'Don't!'"

I remember clearly my own feelings as a single adult (I was single until age thirty) after hearing references in sermons about single sexuality. The aftertaste was kind of bitter. The married man or woman preaching the sermon made sense, but it made me a bit angry that he or she could go home that night and be sexually active. Many times I heard singles remark, "Well, it's easy for him [or her] to say!" And even worse, nothing positive was mentioned about being sexual as a single person. I remember struggling with this for years, thinking that there was a huge, gaping hole in the whole theology of single sexuality. I often thought, *I know what God doesn't want me to do, but what does He want me to do? There must be a positive side to single sexuality.*

GOD IS NOT AFRAID TO TELL US WHY

Many couples have told me that the only instruction they were given as to why they should abstain before marriage was simply, "The Bible says that it is wrong." Of course, that is a good reason—a very good reason. But singles are adults, not children, and they desire sufficient explanations to be given along with caring instructions. Singles are not satisfied with "I told you so"; they want to know why they should remain celibate until the wedding night, and they search for adult answers.

Don't get me wrong here—I'm not against obedience, and neither are singles who desire to live out their Christianity. However, the "obedience only" approach does not help many singles handle their sexuality well. In conversations with hundreds of singles, I have discovered that Christian singles want to be obedient to God, but they are also searching for a deeper reason to be temporarily celibate than mere obedience. It's not that obedience is wrong; it just needs to be buttressed by reasons why one should obey. It's OK for parents to say, "Because I said so," to a young child; but when that child becomes a teen and then finally an adult, "Because I said so" is insufficient.

For those who are still virgins, a positive approach can be quite a help. Jaclyn, a twenty-two-year-old virgin, wrote,

I never had the problem of going too far with a guy, because I refused to put myself in a situation where I would. It usually meant that relationships fizzled out quickly, and as much as that hurt, I knew that if I would have started any type of sexual activity, each time we would have gone just a little bit farther. That type of intimacy in a relationship really frightened me too. I was always afraid of getting pregnant or a sexually transmitted disease. Fear was a good motivation to remain abstinent.

It seems, however, that the older I get, the more I want that intimacy with a man. Not so much sex, but intimacy. A part of me wants immediate gratification; the other part of me knows the value of purity. I also know that once any type of sexual activity begins and limits are set, they can always be (and probably will be) broken.

Jaclyn then described the fresh perspective she found in my statement "Purity is directly related to personal worth." She wrote:

I never realized that because I have remained sexually pure, I am of personal value. Taking it a step further, because I'm of value personally, I look at myself as being more valuable in God's eyes as well.

"Celibacy is a way of protecting and asserting (her) worth" is my favorite statement. By not giving into sexual desires when I'm involved with someone (which is getting more and more difficult), I realized I was telling my partner, myself, and God that I'm worth more than a cheap thrill or momentary gratification."

Jaclyn discovered what, I believe, God wants every person, whether married or single, to learn about sexuality. God doesn't just want to give us the rules and force us to obey mindlessly. He does not desire that we remain infants, but He truly wants us to grow into spiritual adulthood. That's why His commands make sense. There are always reasons behind His injunctions; for every command, there is a corresponding rationale. God is not afraid to treat us as adults. There is a sufficient answer to the "Why wait?" question.

Christian singles deeply need this positive *why* behind God's instructions on single sexuality. If you are single, only a clear and convincing positive *why* will give you the needed strength to resolve to remain temporarily celibate. Without this positive why, you may not have the willpower to withstand the temptations of our sexually supercharged society. Willpower alone doesn't seem to be an adequate motivation to avoid premarital sex.

Furthermore, if you're a youth minister or parent, you need a new approach to help teens and college students have positive reasons to remain celibate until marriage. If you are in such a leadership position, you have a unique opportunity—you can help kids learn this early in their lives, before they devalue themselves sexually. How wonderful it would be if youth could learn at an early stage the positive reason to wait until marriage.

Visit any Christian store that sells books on sexuality that are against pre-marital sexual activity. You will find the books are of high quality, biblically correct, and largely negative when it comes to single sexuality. As an unmarried person, you probably will feel strangely un-satisfied. The reason may be the approach. Most authors will give one of three warnings against premarital sex: (1) "Don't, because God says 'no.' If you obey, He will bless you someday" (this is the approach that emphasizes God's rules, principles, and guidelines for Christian living); (2) "Don't, because it will hurt you later after you are married" (the divorce rate is higher, the marital satisfaction is lower, etc.); or (3) "Don't, because of the risk of AIDS and other sexual diseases." For instance, Kay Kuzma, in her book *When You're Serious About Love: Straight talk to Single Adults,* lists twenty reasons why premarital sex is wrong—all of them negative (pp. 120–33). Paul Reiser, M.D., in the Focus on the Family booklet *Sex and Singles: Reasons to Wait,* stresses the medical and pregnancy dangers that one risks with premarital sex. Dick Purnell, in a chapter called "Say Yes and Be Sorry" from his book *Becoming a Friend and a Lover,* lists twenty-three negative conse-quences to sex before marriage.

Of course, all of these are helpful books, and the dangers they identify are real. My point is simply that singles need more than dangers and fear to motivate them; they need the positive side of single sexuality.

NEEDED: A POSITIVE APPROACH TO SINGLE SEXUALITY

All of these approaches are based on truth, yet they need supple-mentation because they motivate from a negative position of law, fear, or guilt. They are unable to say more, because they lack a positive theology for single sexuality. Furthermore, singles today—indeed all adults in our modern culture—have difficulty living totally in the future. "What if I never get married?" singles ask. "What about the present? What does God want me to do with my sexuality now that would be positive?"

Christian leaders would like to believe that singles in their churches are not sexually active, but the truth is that many singles are (as the statistics in chapter 5 will show). If you are a church leader, just ask some singles—they will tell you that there's a lot of fooling around going on (of course, there is a lot of that among the marrieds too, unfortunately). Then ask the singles how they feel about their sexuality. Most Christian singles will admit they feel guilty, confused, and hypocritical. It matters not whether they are sexually active or celibate; even those singles who are not sexually active feel guilty, confused, and hypocritical because of their strong desires. They aren't doing it, but they would like to, which is why they don't feel fulfilled either.

Without a positive reason to abstain, the celibate life is extremely difficult for singles. It seems contrary to our natural inclinations. To live as a celibate adult seems to violate our biological design and oppose our bodies' desires. For most single adults, being unable to express our sexuality in a fully physical way is as difficult as putting a harness on our hormones. A positive reason for single sexuality can help enormously.

GOD'S SURPRISE FOR SINGLES

It is my hope and prayer that a new, positive approach to single Christian sexuality will fill an empty hole in the lives of almost eighty million single adults in the United States, many of whom are looking for answers. Whether divorced, bereaved, engaged, or just looking for quality friendships, a positive approach to single sexuality will enrich life. Although this approach will be most easily accessible to Christians, it also will help non-Christians and may even provide a reason for nonbelievers to be temporarily celibate besides the fear of AIDS or pregnancy.

God has a surprising "yes" that speaks to Christian singles. By approaching single sexuality in terms of value, whole new dimensions of meaning and fulfillment are open to singles.

Questions for Discussion
1. The "Singles Speaks" quote told of a man who was taught about sexuality in a very negative way. Were you taught about sexuality in a positive or negative way? Can you give any examples?
2. Why do you think "I told you so" is a weak motivator? Is it a weak motivator if God is the speaker?
3. Do you think Christians are comfortable talking about their sexuality? Why or why not? Who are more uncomfortable talking about their sexuality—married Christians or single Christians?
4. Before we jump into the "value" approach to sexuality, list a few things that you value. Why do you value them?

CHAPTER TWO

HOW MUCH ARE SINGLES WORTH SEXUALLY?

THE SIX HUNDRED DOLLAR TABLE

A middle-aged woman named Pearl had owned an antique store for several years. Her showroom included a special antique table that had been there a long time. Because Pearl needed more room and wanted to move some merchandise around, she decided to sell the table at a discount. The price tag was marked $500. She crossed out the $500 with her marking pen and wrote, "Sale $400."

Later that day a man came in and saw the table with the price marked down. After introducing himself as Ted, he tried to bargain with her, saying, "I'll tell you what, I'll buy that table for $300."

Pearl responded, "$300! Oh, no. It's worth a lot more than that. This table is worth more than $1,000. You would be getting a truly great deal for only $400."

"But it's got scratches on it!" Ted replied.

"It's an antique. Antiques have had a lot of use."

"But I'll have to refinish it when I get home," he countered.

"It's made of solid oak. They don't make tables like this anymore," she said, making a good point.

Back and forth they went. He kept trying to convince her to lower the price, and she kept giving reasons why it was worth more.

Finally Ted said, "You know, I'd buy this table if you would just change the price."

With a grin, Pearl said, "Well, OK. Talking to you has convinced me that I should change the price after all." She took her marking pen, crossed out the $400 price, and wrote above it, "$600."

Ted was shocked. "Hold it, you can't do that," he screamed.

"What do you mean I can't do that? I own this table. I can sell it for any price I want."

"But you had it marked for $400."

"Yes, but talking to you has helped me see the real value of this table. Our discussion has reminded me how special this table is and that it is worth much more than $400. I realized that if I sold it for $400, I would be cheating myself—I'd actually be getting less than I deserved. Someday someone will realize how valuable it is. If not, I'll still own a great table. So thanks for reminding me how valuable this table is."

Ted thought for a moment and then said, "OK, you win. I can see you are quite a saleswoman. I'll tell you what. I'll buy this table for $400."

"Oh, no, you won't," Pearl said firmly. "It's not for sale for $400. I will take nothing less than $600 for this table, and that is still a great bargain on a wonderfully special table."

Once again Ted became angry. He sulked and complained as he walked around the store. But eventually he bought that antique table for $600.

A BARGAIN TABLE GETS BARGAIN TREATMENT

The "Six Hundred Dollar Table" is one of my favorite true stories, told to me by a single woman whose name really was Pearl. It has become one of the most useful tools in counseling single adults that I have ever discovered. In vivid terms, the $600 table story illustrates just what happens in human relationships.

Singles quickly understand that the way the table gets treated depends on the price it is sold for—and they make the connection that the treatment they receive in relationships depends on the value they place on themselves. For instance, consider if Ted had paid only $300. After he had owned the table two weeks, one of his children places a glass of water on the table, leaving a ring. What's his reaction? *Oh, no big deal,* he thinks. *It's not a very expensive table. It doesn't have a very good finish anyway.* But if Ted had paid $600 for the table, he will snatch the glass immediately from the child's hand and say, "Don't put the glass on the table without using a coaster! This is a valuable table—I paid $600 for it. Treat it well."

The same is true in relationships. The kind of treatment we receive is directly related to how cheaply we sell ourselves or what kind of treatment we hold out for. If we allow ourselves to be treated poorly, we will receive poor treatment. If we hold out for better treatment, we will eventually receive it.

Sharon (not her real name) was a lovely single woman who was tired of dating—and even worse, marrying—men that she called "losers." It became clear to me that Sharon longed to find a man who would treat her well, but she saw no connection between the way she was treated and the way she allowed herself to be treated. After listening for a while, I leaned forward in my chair and said, "Do you mind if I share with you one of my favorite stories?"

Sharon brightened up and said, "Go ahead."

So I began, "Let me tell you the story of the 'Six Hundred Dollar Table.'"

Sharon enjoyed the story, and the discussion that followed. I asked her, "If the saleswoman had decided to accept the $300 offer from the man, would she have ever received $600 for the table?"

Sharon, slightly confused, thought for a moment and eventually said, "Well, no, of course she wouldn't. Once she sold it for $300, it would be gone; so she couldn't get more later."

As she immediately realized for herself, the same is true in any relationship between two people. Once we sell our goods for a certain price, we will never know if someone might later have offered more.

As another way of illustrating this point, I asked Sharon to imagine that she found a great deal and bought a home for $100,000 cash. "If you then decided to sell that house for $100,000, and someone came along who wanted to buy it but only offered $1,000, would you accept that offer?"

"Of course not," she replied.

"How about an offer of $5,000?"

"No."

"How about $25,000? How about $50,000 or $80,000?"

"We're getting closer, but still no sale."

"You wouldn't sell for $80,000? Why not?" I said.

"You're getting warmer," Sharon said, "but I still would hold out for the full price. After all, I paid good money for it! Sooner or later, someone will want that house for the full price; if not, I'm better off keeping it than taking less than it's worth."

"Sharon," I cautiously suggested, "it's fascinating to me that we treat our physical possessions better than we treat ourselves. We will wait for the full price of what a car, a house, or a condo is worth, because we know how valuable that item is. But when it comes to our own self-worth, we seem to be unsure of our own value and give ourselves away at a much cheaper rate. We sell ourselves at discount prices and receive much less than we are worth."

That's the first point of the $600 table story. If we sell ourselves cheaply, we will not be treated in accordance with our full value. Pearl couldn't go back to Ted later and say, "I realize that the antique table was worth more. Pay me another $300." Ted would laugh and say, "Forget it! We made a deal. The table is mine."

Sometimes in relationships we try to do the same thing. After selling ourselves cheaply in the beginning, we realize that we are worth more; so we bring up the sensitive topic of discussion—"You know, I would like you to treat me better than you have been."

But seldom do such appeals or requests work. After all, that would be changing the terms of the contract. And after a man or a woman has been able to use something cheaply for a while, he or she will naturally be hesitant to pay more for the same product or service.

The point is clear: Once we give ourselves away cheaply, we will not experience the treatment that is equal to what we are worth.

WHAT KIND OF TREATMENT DO YOU WANT?

My favorite part of the discussion about the $600 table, though, occurs after the second question: "When Ted bought that antique table for $600 and brought it home later that night, do you think he treated it like a $300 table or a $600 table?"

At this Sharon smiled, leaned back in her chair, and said, "Oh, now I see where you are going with this story. I'll bet he treated it like a $600 table. Right?"

Before answering, I further questioned, "But how do you think he would have treated it if he had only paid $300?"

"He would've treated it like a $300 table," Sharon answered,

Finally we had arrived at the crucial point of the illustration. "But what's the difference?" I asked, "It's the same table; yet in one instance it's treated like it's worth only $300, the other instance like it's worth $600?"

The answer was clear for Sharon, as it has been to thousands of singles who have heard this true story—it's not the value the man placed on the table that mattered most. Instead, it's the worth the saleswoman put on the table, and held out for, that determined how the man would treat the table.

After I tell that story, many single adults realize that it is their view of themselves that determines how others will treat them. At this point, I simply ask, "Now tell me, if you were a table, how much would you be worth? Would you be a $300 table, a $400 table, a $500 table, or a $600 table?"

Some say, "I feel like a $10 table. I have given myself away so cheaply and have been treated so poorly that I feel worthless." Others say, "I guess about $300. I'm not going to end up in a thrift store, but I will never receive full price either. I will never be treated like I would like to be." Still others smile and say, "I'm a $600 table, and I have been waiting a long time for someone to discover and treat me like that."

When I asked Sharon to put a price on her table, she laughed a sort of sad laugh and said her table was worth about 50¢. It was a painful, poignant moment for both of us.

Then I asked: "Sharon, do you know what kind of a table God thinks you are? Do you know how valuable you are in God's sight?"

Sharon thought for a minute and hesitatingly said, "Well, you're probably going to say that in God's eyes, I'm a $600 table."

"Oh, no," I replied, "God thinks you are worth much more than that. The Bible says God so loved the world—that means you—that He gave His one and only Son. That means in God's eyes, you are worth so much that He gave Jesus, His only child, for you. God loves you so much that we can't put a monetary value on it, but in a metaphorical way we can say you are not a $600 table—you are a million dollar table!"

SETTING THE PRICE TAGS

As the story of the $600 table clearly illustrates, the treatment we receive as individuals is directly related to the value we place upon ourselves. People will not naturally treat us poorly because they view us as cheap. The big surprise is that often the way others treat us is a product of our own choosing. We ourselves select the type of treatment we will continue to receive from others. If we do not value ourselves, we probably will allow others to treat us poorly. On the other hand, if we truly value ourselves, we will not settle for poor treatment. In many instances, the prices that others have paid for us were not set by others—we filled in the price tags ourselves.

This has enormous implications for single sexuality. If we want to be treated as valuable sexually, we have to first believe that we are valuable sexually. Conversely, if we are treated poorly sexually, it may be because we do not view ourselves as physically valuable. The way we are treated will often follow from the way we view ourselves.

Unfortunately, our culture has this completely backwards. Movies, TV shows, and probably your friends teach that you are valuable sexually only if you can find someone who will treat you as valuable. Thus, if we can find such a person, it proves that we are of special worth. If we cannot find anyone like that, we conclude that we can't be very valuable after all.

Contrary to the prevailing message of our culture that free sex will make us feel good, it actually causes us to feel bad about ourselves. What's worse, the feelings of regret sometimes last a lifetime and can actually inhibit sexual enjoyment later in marriage. Read one man's story in "A Single Speaks." Though it may seem extreme, the sad news is that it's probably close to the norm today, for pressure for sexual involvement often begins even prior to high school. Indeed, many young people today have their first sexual experience in *grade school*. That, too, can cause us to devalue something of great value, our sexual being.

A SINGLE SPEAKS

Aside from playing doctor as a child, my first sexual experience was in sixth grade with a girl who sat next to me in class. We played little 'sex dare' games by grabbing each other underneath the desk we shared. We decided we were 'too cool' to remain virgins. So we met after school and climbed over a wall into a secluded place. We took off our pants, and I had an erection. I was scared and excited. We didn't really know how to have sex. I touched her breasts (which looked about the same as mine), and then we touched genitals. We decided that we had "done it" and were no longer virgins. I ran home and did not tell anyone.

Then I discovered my father's porno-box of books and magazines, and I masturbated frequently from that time on. I did not like my father's pornography because it was sado-masochistic; I had to sift through it to find the parts that I liked . . .

I dated and necked but never had sex or oral sex until I was 17 and dating the girl who would eventually become my wife. Our relationship progressed and we were 'in love.' We necked, petted, and within three months were having oral sex. About four to six months later, we actually had sexual intercourse . . . we broke up after one year and six months.

During the last months of our relationship, I had sex with two other girls and oral sex with another. I knew my relationship with God and my girlfriend were very bad, and I decided to change. Two weeks after rededicating my life to God, my girlfriend broke up with me.

I was devastated when we broke up because I really loved this girl. I hurt deeper because of the intensity of the sexual relationship. I felt like part of my soul had been ripped out.

I was in my second year of college, and I had not gotten another girlfriend. I was trying to change my ways, but I found it much more difficult to avoid sexual relationships after having been in one. I had sex with two girls during this time—one-time deals. I called it 'friendship sex' since neither of us had any intentions of a relationship beyond friendship. I struggled with this. I knew I was a huge flirt, but these girls were very aggressive. I felt seduced, although willingly.

I then changed my circle of friends and made the changes necessary to not . . . put myself in sexual situations. I dated a girl in my junior year of college whom I thought I loved. We were not the right match, but we tried. About three months into the relationship, she pressured me to have sex with her. She told me that sex and love went together, and that if I really loved her I would make love to her, so I decided I wanted to do that. Our relationship changed after that. Sex became the intimacy, and the real relationship faded out. After nine months, we broke up . . .

[After three years of dating various women,] I began dating my first girlfriend again. We had both changed, and our commitment to God was real. Now we are married, and I have regrets: (1) the influence of pornography on my thoughts and sexual desires, and (2) my past sexual partners, who were not my wife, that I sometimes think about."

A MILLION DOLLAR WOMAN WHO ACCEPTED A FIFTY DOLLAR TREATMENT

Donna is an example of a woman who looked to others to provide her with an assessment of her worth. Donna matured early physically and had plenty of attention from boys, especially older boys. As a freshman in high school, she dated a popular senior. How special she felt. He wasn't perfect, but he was certainly better than she had hoped for. When she was with him, she felt like a queen. Actually, that feeling was more the result of her fantasy than the way he treated her, because he wasn't mature enough to treat her really well, as she would later realize. Yet he was her first boyfriend, and that was enough.

It was a real boost to her ego to be the only freshman at the Senior Ball, but she quickly realized there was a price to be paid for her popularity. She discovered that she was not popular with everybody. The senior girls treated her like a pariah. The other senior boys weren't genuinely friendly either. Her popularity was limited to the one boy she dated and the other freshman girls who looked on her with awe.

But there was a price to be paid even for those friends. The boy had to be indulged not only socially but also sexually—he basically called the shots and Donna went along for the ride. He wasn't interested in what she wanted to do or who she was deep inside. Her dating life looked exciting on the outside, but from the inside it was empty and superficial. In spite of this, she still felt special. Although the focus in their sexual relationship was on him, she felt wanted. After all, he was her first partner, and she naively assumed that she was also his first (she was too embarrassed to ask).

Her friendships with the other freshman girls weren't much better. Her whole status was built on her relationship with her boyfriend, so she felt unable to share her real feelings of frustration and isolation with her friends. If they really knew that her claim to fame wasn't that great after all, she wondered if they would like her anymore. So she was silent and kept her pain inside, although on the outside she "had it all."

As a sophomore in high school, Donna was introduced to a college crowd, so her dates and steady boyfriends were almost exclusively college men. Of course, this further separated her from her high school friends, and gradually her life became more and more removed from her own high school. Naturally, her college boyfriends looked down on her few remaining high school friends, and eventually on Donna for still being in high school. With little in common, Donna and her college men didn't talk about much. Instead, they kissed a lot, necked for hours, and experimented with the joys (?) promised by the sexual revolution.

In time, Donna realized she no longer felt special. Even though she knew she was pretty and sexually attractive, she began to feel more and more worthless. As she said, "I was really confused at that time in my life. The men treated me very special before asking me out and also at the beginning of a date, but I didn't feel very special at the end. It wasn't that they treated me poorly. I had great dates who showed me lots of attention and spent lots of money. I think it was that I was sexually involved with so many of them. After a while, I just felt cheap."

Yet Donna didn't consider herself a loose girl. After all, she had certain standards and wouldn't sleep with just anyone. She wasn't a prostitute; she didn't do drugs; she wasn't into kinky things. Yet she was deeply unhappy and confused. If men thought she was special, why didn't she feel special anymore?

This feeling of worthlessness became even stronger in college. Night after night, Donna would attend a party or go out on a date, but the next morning would feel strangely numb, as if a dentist had injected her whole body—maybe her soul—with Novocain. She had several steady boyfriends during this time, but the gnawing feelings of worthlessness persisted.

In her senior year, she began to think that maybe her feelings of worthlessness could be solved by getting married. If she could be married and build a family with just one man, then she would feel special again. Eventually, her boyfriend Jerry asked her to marry him, and she eagerly accepted. Both of them were thrilled. Donna would finally have the stability she longed for and would start to feel valuable again. Jerry could not believe his good luck. Donna was the most beautiful woman he had ever dated, and the idea of marrying her was beyond his wildest dreams.

With their parents' approval, they married soon after graduation. They both found good jobs, established a comfortable home, and eventually grew to love each other with a more mature, lasting love. However, Donna was unable to shake her feelings of worthlessness. In spite of the fact that she was now happily married, socially respectable, and financially stable, she felt that gnawing sense of worthlessness. *What's wrong with me?* she asked herself.

Jerry also became frustrated. Try as he might, he could not convince her that he really loved her, that she was extremely valuable in his sight. In time, he started doubting himself, thinking that part of the problem was that he was not a good husband. But he also knew that the fault was partly Donna's. It was almost as if she wanted to be loved above all else but was unable to let anyone love her. Many times Jerry asked himself, *What's wrong?*

THE ROOT PROBLEM

Donna's problem was deep and complex. Some may say that Donna's problem was in her expectations. Really, they say, "An individual is not that special after all. We are just a higher form of animal life that longs for transcendence but can never find it." As the popular saying goes, "Live for today, because tomorrow you die." If there really is no God and no afterlife, there also is no way to escape from the desperate sense of meaningless and worthlessness inherent in being a finite human. Yet Donna knew people who did feel a sense of transcendence, who did feel special and valuable. *If life is truly without value or meaning, wouldn't it be so for everyone?* she wondered.

Others will claim that Donna's problem was simply lack of self-esteem, and they are partly right. Donna did not feel very valuable. Some would suggest that she should enter therapy. Maybe she should

read some self-help books and begin to think positively. Like The Little
Engine That Could, maybe she should repeat to herself, in mantra-like
fashion, "I think I'm special, I think I'm special, I think I'm special."
Such self-help approaches miss the heart of the problem—the root of
her lack of self-esteem, indeed the root of much of the lack of self-
esteem in our contemporary culture.

My contention is that many feelings of low self-esteem and worthlessness have their root in a physical/sexual dimension. Obviously, our
physical and emotional selves are intimately connected, so it should be
no surprise that how we allow ourselves to be valued physically will
influence how we appraise ourselves emotionally, mentally, and spiritually.

This is a hard concept, but here's a simple illustration that shows
how we value ourselves will affect how we allow ourselves to be treated. Let's look again at the $600 table to gain new insight into the root
cause of Donna's problem.

Donna gave herself away sexually (cheaply) for years. She was
treated like a $50 table. Over and over, she would settle for a price
much beneath her real worth, until finally she came to believe that the
low price was her real worth. Because others viewed her as a $50
table, and she went along with their appraisal, she finally came to believe that she didn't have much worth.

Later, when her husband, who thought she was a $1,000 table,
tried to treat her like someone especially valuable, she had a hard time
accepting that. Donna had allowed herself to be treated cheaply for so
long that the conclusion that she was indeed cheap burned itself into her
mind, even into her very soul. She was like a computer screen that is
left on too long—the image burns itself into a permanent image on the
screen, so that even if other programs are called up, the burned-in
image still faintly shows through all other images. For Donna, that image had distorted all future images by its lingering presence.

Like Donna, many single adults have looked to others to set the
price for their own sexuality, and in the process they have burned into
their souls an appraisal that is far below their real value. Their thinking
goes like this: *If others treat me as though I'm valuable, then I must be.
But if others treat me cheaply, then it must really prove that I'm not valuable after all.*

Who taught us that we should base our feelings of personal worth
upon how others treat us? Our relationships, like Donna's, mirror what
we already think about ourselves. We have each set our own price
tags. The sexual revolution simply "gave permission" to those already
vulnerable to sexual involvement. In the next chapter, we will consider

the destructiveness of the sexual revolution to those who have difficulty feeling worthy.

Questions for Discussion

1. Which person in the table story did you identify with most, Pearl or Ted? Why?
2. What determines the value of a table? Is it the salesperson's opinion, the manufacturer's, the buyer's, or a combination? Why?
3. Shouldn't Pearl have just taken the $300? After all, "a bird in the hand is worth two in the bush."
4. Do you think Ted got a good deal? How about Pearl?
5. If you were a table, what kind of price tag would you place on yourself right now? $50, $100, $300, $600, $1,000, $1,000,000? How valuable do you feel? Why?
6. Think back on a time in your life when someone treated you poorly. Is it possible that you were treated poorly because you did not value yourself highly and sold yourself cheaply? Share your experience.

CHAPTER THREE

WHY DO SINGLES SOMETIMES FEEL WORTHLESS?

The sexual revolution loudly proclaimed that there was no reason to wait. As Crosby, Stills, and Nash sang "Love the One You're With," the baby boomer generation listened with rapt attention and gave it a try. Sex outside of marriage became a very common event in some age groups, maybe even more common than sex within marriage.

Sex was not seen as something to save for marriage but was something to use freely, regardless of marital status. Movie stars openly talked about their live-in partners, and living together before marriage lost its moral stigma. Living together meant sharing an apartment and sharing bodies. The moral theme of the '70s and '80s was the same as the economic theme: don't save—spend.

There was a problem with this indiscriminate use of sexuality. Though people appeared to be sexually free, they were neither sexually nor emotionally fulfilled. They sowed their wild oats but reaped a very poor harvest. For millions of Americans, the sexual revolution has not paid a good return on their investment.

THE RESULTS OF CASUAL SEX

The sexual revolution promised happiness, freedom, and intimacy, but the real result was the gradual cheapening of a sense of personal value and a sense of sexual value among single adults—and even among married adults who were sexually permissive before marriage.

This is the conclusion of many who lived through the sexual revolution. In the article "The New Chastity" in *Cosmopolitan* magazine, Carolyn See wrote, "Sex is supposed to be fun, freeing . . . yet too many partners can sometimes make you feel disconsolate, unsatisfied. Why are so many young women suddenly swearing off the world of 'junk food' sex?" Her question reflects the trivializing of this important physical act. (And as we shall soon see, the problem is much deeper and more painful than a mere feeling of dissatisfaction.)

This kind of question surprises us, especially that it would be asked in *Cosmopolitan*. But Carolyn See is right on the mark. Sexual promiscuity is not the wonderful lifestyle it is hyped up to be. Sleeping around is not the exotic life of the rich and famous, and it is not Disneyland. Even if there were no sexual diseases and an AIDS crisis, sex without commitment is still far from problem-free. It is, at base, damaging to the soul. See points this out in an candid yet insightful way:

> What does all this mean in a discussion of the new chastity? What it means, I think, is that despite the Pill, legalized abortion, and economic freedom, our bodies are trying to tell us something: They don't necessarily want to be tossed around like lost luggage on a round-the-world plane trip. That's why, maybe, after a long night of good times . . . with a Nick Nolte look-alike . . . you go out for coffee in the kitchen, and something, someplace in your body feels like if it could cry, it would cry. It's not your genitalia feeling bad, it may not even be your "heart." It's in the vicinity of your lungs, your solar plexus, where some Eastern religions suggest your soul resides. In other words, recreational sex is not soul food.[1]

See develops this theme further, illustrating it with vivid imagery and examples:

> Yet, however difficult the choice, after close to two decades of sexual permissiveness (what a tiresome phrase; one gets "permission" to go to the cloakroom in grade school, not to go to bed with darling men!), more and more young women are opting for the new chastity. . . . "What's all this stuff about the new chastity?" asks a beautiful showgirl who was once married to a famous tap dancer. "I'm still working on the old kind! Save yourself for a man you love or at least one who makes your heart flutter. Otherwise it's meat loaf, under brand X catsup."[2]

See is right again. The indiscriminate use of sexuality ends up making a person feel overused and rundown. Many singles feel like a worn-out suitcase, battered and torn from too many miles logged. In her words, sexually active singles feel like "lost luggage on a round-the-world plane trip," used, worn out, and cheap. Sexual experiences do not reinforce a person's ultimate value and importance. Singles who give themselves sexually feel depreciated, marked-down in price. They feel valueless. No longer are they treated like prime rib; now they are just meat loaf under generic catsup. What an image—but how it fits reality and reveals the consequences of the meat-market mentality toward sex.

Read "A Single Speaks." How easy it is to confuse sex with love, and how easy it is to sell ourselves cheaply.

A SINGLE SPEAKS

At 18, I knew that I was the only living female out of all my friends who remained boyfriendless. I felt left out, alone, and terribly abnormal. Then it finally happened. I began 'seeing,' or so we called it then, an older man (he was 19 and out of high school, so that impressed all my friends).

From the beginning things went kind of fast—we were kissing after about a week and three phone conversations. This didn't bother me, though, because I felt that I had waited so long that I didn't want to miss any more of what all my friends had told me about. After two weeks, we were hanging out alone at his house and 'watching' *Gone with the Wind*. The action did not stop at just kissing but escalated to petting or fondling. I was raised a non-Christian, but sex to me was still something I felt should be saved for marriage. Though this activity was taking place, each of us remained fully clothed; so I felt that nothing was lost. I was wrong.

At this time, my friends were my sole source of encouragement and support because my relationship with my family was not exactly close. I shared everything with my friends, and they encouraged me to give in and become a 'real woman.' I didn't want them to think I was a baby or was not able to keep a boyfriend around. I was torn between my feelings of wanting to remain pure, the peer pressure, and also my curiosity to find out about what the fuss was all about. Not only that, but my hormones and my body went crazy every time he and I were together (I thought it had to be love).

As the weeks went on, the touching became more intimate, and he would try to get me to give in. I remained firm in my stance for about a month, but on prom night I became intoxicated and gave in. We continued to have intercourse for about two months after this—at which point the guilt became too much, and I told him I couldn't do it anymore.

I felt dirty, ashamed, and deceitful, but my friends were really proud and envious of me and our great relationship. I was again torn between what I knew was right and keeping him happy and around. I decided to go with what I knew was right. After all, he loved me, right?

Wrong! I found out where his heart really was when I found out he was seeing a girl he worked with, because she would give him what he wanted. I was devastated. My life turned upside down because not only was he dumping me, but I could never again save myself for the man I would marry. I decided that since I was impure anyway I might as well have a good time with it. For three years I gave myself freely to whomever I thought might be the least bit interested—not one-night stands but in relationships. None of them worked for longer than two months because they wanted sex, but I wanted love.

Finally after three years of grieving and trying to get back at him, I found a place to heal. A friend introduced me to Jesus. What a difference He made in my life! I stopped hanging out in bars, drinking, and looking for trouble. I began to turn my entire life over to Him. I left all my old friends and habits behind and began to make new ones. I became involved in a church ministry with toddlers and really desired to be different. I wasn't presented with the opportunity for sexual contact in any way and was relieved and happy.

After two years, I was offered a position as a youth worker. . . . [Soon] my own past came to haunt me. I began to remember things I had done years ago and began to feel dirty once again. I could not forgive myself for giving away something that was not only mine but was also God's. If I couldn't forgive me, then God certainly couldn't.

This became the hardest time in my life. I began to feel that I had no place in the ministry and that I could never be effective. Guilt and remorse from the past consumed me, and I began to withdraw. I finally mustered up the courage to approach an older lady, both chronologically and in the Lord. She was able to show me Scripture about God forgiving all sin and making us new creations. She encouraged me to remain in the ministry as a vessel for God to use from the growth that this situation could bring.

I remained in the ministry with youth, and more than once have encouraged those who felt unforgiven and were torn between holding out and giving in. I told them to save their one-time gift for the one-time day."

WITH LITTLE VALUE

Of course, many of us know what the Bible teaches: sex outside marriage is not good soul food. But we had to discover this truth for ourselves, just as we seem to need to learn most things in the "school of hard knocks." Now, finally, the lesson has been learned. A life of sensuality is all give and no take; it is all withdrawals and no deposits. The sexual revolution has left many in our culture in extreme poverty;

its impact on the value of life has been devastating. People feel used and discarded. Their value has been forfeited.

Many singles, both men and women, have experienced this feeling of devaluation in their sexual experiences. Years of sexual splurging and unrestrained behavior have left them empty and unfulfilled. Even worse, they have spent all they had—given up all that was meant to be cherished—and have received nothing in return. In the process, they have suffered the tragic consequences of singles who abandon celibacy. They cheapen themselves. As Frank, an attractive man who had lived too long in the fast lane, admitted, "It's no big deal to go to bed with a woman anymore. I've been to bed so many times that I've lost count of the women. It's not special anymore. Anyone that wants me pretty much gets me."

Jerome expressed the same feeling of worthlessness as he described a certain role he had to play while dating. "To tell you the truth, I feel cheapened by the dating process. I mean, in order to get a woman to spend time with me, I have to spend a wad of money. Most women won't give me the time of day unless I pay. How valuable does that make me feel? I feel like a guy who can't get a woman on his own charms, so he has to pay for a [service]. I'm not even a $50 table—I'm a negative $50 table! It costs me to find company!"

Jerome is obviously frustrated by the cultural pressure on men to be the ones who treat the other as valuable, but often don't feel valuable in return. The very process, he claims, chips away at his self-worth. In a strange coincidence, Frank has also had his self-worth depreciated by the women he dates. What Jerome and Frank are really saying is that they do not feel very valuable. Through his physical intimacy, Frank has been used so much that he feels worthless. He does not feel like a costly gem or a valuable treasure, but a piece of costume jewelry. Through the spending of his money, Jerome feels unappreciated and unwanted for who he is as a person.

Through different actions, both men feel they are held in little esteem by women. Unfortunately, both men and women are victims of the same process—the gradual erosion of feelings of personal worth in our culture.

This experience of sexual and personal worthlessness is common not only for singles who have never married but also for those who were formerly married. For many who have been through the pain of divorce, there is often a corresponding pain in the sexual arena. When divorcing couples begin to harm one another emotionally, that often is communicated sexually as well. This is a seldom talked about consequence of divorce.

Shirley found herself inflicting pain on herself as well as her husband as she considered a divorce. She wrote at the end of a seminar, "I married a full-time Christian worker during Bible college. I was a virgin. My background was very legalistic, along with my schooling, which led to entering a relationship in which we really didn't know each other. After staying in a lousy marriage for nine years, I am finally in the process of a divorce. Toward the end of my marriage, I became sexually involved with a man who was also married whom I love and says he loves me. After finding out that I was pregnant for the first time in my life, the pressure and stress became unbearable. I was still teaching in a Christian school, and my husband was still working as a youth pastor. We opted for the 'easy' way out—abortion.

"This is a decision that both of us have regretted on a daily basis. I have experienced severe depression and eating disorders because of the emotional trauma of living a lie, dealing with a lousy marriage, facing disappointed parents because of my divorce, and an abortion—all of which I never planned."

When love starts to wane or resentments grow, one of the first things to go is sexual intimacy. Michelle, an attractive but overweight thirty-five-year-old, said, "Our marriage was shaky for many years, but I knew it was really in trouble when he refused my sexual advances— something he had begged me to do for years. One night he said, 'Forget it. Your fat doesn't turn me on.' I knew then that the love was gone for sure. We've been divorced now for five years, and I've lost lots of weight. But I can't shake these feelings of being unattractive sexually."

Michelle's account is not unusual. Couples often cease all physical intimacy years before the actual divorce papers are filed. Many even move into different bedrooms or purchase separate homes. After the divorce, the pain of physical rejection lingers and retains its power.

Another cause for feelings of sexual and personal worthlessness can be the sexual activities of the couple. Some women have been mistreated sexually by their former husbands, and some men have been mistreated by their former wives. In addition, some sexual activities are flagrantly degrading. As one divorcee wrote to me in a confidential note, "I feel stained—green with 'RAPED' written on my heart—damaged, worthless, and ashamed of what's been done to me and what I have done."

Some formerly married people may feel devalued because their spouses never learned the true purpose for the sexual act. *Sexual intimacy is intended to communicate value,* not merely to bring pleasure. When divorced or other single people have been treated as toys instead of the treasures they are, they feel cheap. Again, this is best expressed by a letter from a woman who attended one of my workshops:

Dear Rick,

Your comment regarding low self-worth based on treatment by my ex-spouse during our marriage really explained a dilemma I did not understand for *years*. I did not understand why I felt so worthless, why I wanted to cry and felt so alone and lonely after sexual contact with my husband. I had a very empty feeling and felt there was something wrong with me. My ex-husband would say I was cold and frigid—meanwhile he was having, I found out, several sexual affairs. I now see that his own low self-esteem was coloring any relationship between the two of us. He did not value me, and I felt that low value he placed on me.

This woman expresses the feelings of valuelessness that millions of married people have felt. Her words echo an important truth: poor sexual treatment can lead to feelings of personal and sexual worthlessness. What a great discovery she made in realizing that the low value she felt reflected not her true worth but instead her husband's mistakenly low valuation of her. She felt cheap, but at least she discovered that she felt cheap because of how he acted, not because of who she was. It was from that discovery that her healing process could begin. If you feel of little value after a sexual encounter, recognize that it is not because of who you are, for you have great worth in God's eyes. Your low sense of worth is a direct consequence of the way you allowed yourself to be treated.

Finally, some people feel devalued sexually because of the tragic experience of molestation. Read the following letter of a woman who wrote to me after a seminar:

Thanks for the message about how you value yourself based your sexual history. . . .

My sexual history begins with being [sexually abused] by my father. I don't know at what age it began, but at age 12 I miscarried as a result of it. I prayed that God would help me, and I feel He did in the only way He could by not allowing the pregnancy to continue.

My dad made matters worse for me by divorcing my mom and leaving the family. I had learned to cope within that system. What I couldn't cope with was the abandonment. As a result of my sexual experience and desire to replace my dad, I led a promiscuous life from my early teens. It was the only way I understood that two people of the opposite sex could relate to each other. I had such a poor assessment of my value that I felt bad and guilty having sex with boys, but I didn't know how to stop it and still receive the kind of "love" I thought was normal from my dates.

Early marriage to a man who resembled my dad and behaved
like him was a disaster from the beginning. He was very verbally
and sexually abusive to me. I thought sexual relations were supposed to hurt.

This woman, scarred from her father's molesting of her, endured
the pain until her own husband began to abuse her children. She divorced and years later met a Christian man who began to understand
and value her as a person. As she wrote, "[This] man was different. He
valued me for something more than a sexual encounter, and he helped
me find the Lord. I am now married to him and am blessed for finally
experiencing a healthy marriage, sex life, and serving the Lord as a
couple."

FEELING CONTAMINATED

The sexual revolution, indeed, has left its followers feeling impov-
erished and cheapened. But that is not the only tragic result of profli-
gate behavior. Unrestrained sexual activity has also given single adults
a deep feeling of contamination.

Consider Phil, thirty-nine and a Christian who chose to play by the
rules of the sexual revolution. A high school teacher, Phil grew up in a
conservative Christian home and made his decision to be a Christian as
a young teenager. It naturally followed that he made a decision to remain celibate until marriage; but that decision, as he entered high
school in the early '70s, was difficult to maintain. He was popular and
good looking, in addition to being a gifted athlete and student.

Since he attended both high school and college in a rural area in
the Midwest and was a leader in his church youth groups, he was able
to date young women of like standards. He had some sexual experiences but was always able to steer clear of "the act" and thereby retain
a feeling of technical virginity. Of course, both he and his girlfriends felt
guilty for their actions, but since they were careful to not do what they
had been told not to do, they continued to tell others to "wait," like
them, until marriage. They were virgins in a technical sense only, but
that was acceptable; those trained in legalism are, after all, the best at
finding loopholes.

When his college girlfriend broke up with him at the end of his
senior year, Phil realized that the "wait" would be longer than he had
planned. After moving to the Northwest and entering graduate school,
he began to question whether the wait was worth it, especially when
the first few women he dated pointed out the absurdity of his view

about technical virginity. He discovered that he didn't really know why he should remain a virgin—technically or non-technically.

Because Phil was so capable and handsome, he always had a few women who wanted to be with him. In fact, he was amazed that some of them were more sexually aggressive than he had ever imagined a woman would be. He abandoned his previous commitment for celibacy and gave himself fully to a sexually active lifestyle.

But because he was a Christian, Phil had an inner need to appear moral to himself. His solution was that he could be sexually active, but only with one woman at a time. "What Jesus really wanted to assert morally," Phil said in his educated manner, "was monogamy in a polygamous culture. He really wasn't as concerned with virginity as He was with appearing to be faithful. So he told himself, *Even though I'm sexually active, I still feel I am living congruently as a Christian because I'm sexually monogamous.*

But none of Phil's moral, monogamous relationships lasted. Whenever a relationship became rocky, it was easier for him to abandon it and pursue any number of new available women. To be fair, it wasn't only Phil who gave up on the women; some of the women gave up on him too. But either way, Phil experienced an amazing byproduct of his many sexual escapades.

As Phil admitted to me, "It's getting more and more difficult to find a good sexual partner. It's not that the women aren't pretty or passionate. Instead, the problem is within me! I have been to bed with so many different women that I can't help but compare them to each other, and I end up dissatisfied somehow with each one. It's like I have a hundred video tapes running in my mind, and when I'm with a woman I run the tapes of the other women and compare them in my head. All of this goes on during sex, and sometimes I even forget who I am with.

"I'm like a guy who is addicted to drugs. After trying different kinds of highs, I crave variety. Just one drug loses its kick after a while. I get bored with just one drug. It's almost like I'm addicted to variety.

"My girlfriends figure this out too. They ask me what I like and try to comply, but pretty soon they get tired of all my different requests. Like one woman said to me, 'Phil, I feel that you're not in love with me, but in love with the things I do. You don't need a woman, you need a robot-doll you can program.'

"The sad part is that she was right! I'm afraid that now I will be a bachelor forever because I could never be happy with just one woman. . . . Everyone thinks I'm free and enjoying life. But I'm not free, and I'm not enjoying myself! I'm not happy, but the truth is that I'm stuck."

I wish Phil were the exception today rather than the rule. How many married people are frustrated sexually because their spouse doesn't perform like someone they knew before, met recently, or saw in a movie? How many men wish their wives had bodies more like the women in the *Playboy* centerfolds? How many women fantasize that their husbands would act like the men in the TV soap operas or romance novels? How many married people are burdened by the memories and images of sexual partners other than their spouses?

Phil is a contaminated man—his mind is full of junk that he would like to get rid of, but try as he might he can't take out the trash. Like so many other singles who said yes to the sexual revolution, his unrestrained sexual activity has left him with a deep sense of contamination.

For Paula, the story is different, but the result is the same: feelings of contamination and emptiness. Though Paula, like Phil, was raised in a Christian home and attended church occasionally as a child, as a teenager she thought church was "uncool." She was a Christian, but only nominally. Her school friends, in her opinion, were cool, and they were doing all the cool things: drinking, smoking, partying, and doing drugs. Of course, they also were sexually active.

Since Paula was shapely and fairly attractive, she was popular with this crowd. The boys always wanted to be with her and would show her great amounts of attention. They would buy the drinks and drugs, pick her up in fancy cars, and take care of all the other details. She felt she had to look good, and she loved getting in their cars and receiving the attention.

Of course, she also had to take off her clothes at some point in the evening. But for Paula that was just one other fun thing to do, one more way to feel excitement. She enjoyed sex. She liked the physical closeness with her boyfriends.

She also discovered that sex was extremely important to those boys, and she held the controls. There was a great amount of power in sexuality. She could use it to get not only drugs and drinks but also money and clothes. She could manipulate the boys into doing what she wanted and going where she desired, just by using her sexual controls. She could even catch any boyfriend she wanted; sex was the ultimate and unfailing bait.

In college Paula caught one guy that she thought was especially great. She put on the charm, cast out her fishing line, and then quickly reeled him in. Soon they were engaged and then married. They enjoyed their sexual life together, yet the marriage ended after a few years; he just could not stand her subtle attempts to manipulate him. Paula became a divorced woman.

She soon learned that the bar scene was surprisingly similar to her former high school scene. The relationships were shallow, and the deceptions ran deep. Her old manipulation techniques worked perfectly, and her calendar soon was filled with adoring men. Life was very exciting, but she was tiring of thrills. Paula longed for lasting love, for someone to truly treasure her. She eventually met and married another man but again ended up divorced.

Now in her mid-thirties, she began to despair of ever having a truly happy marriage. It seemed as if she attracted the wrong type of men—men who just used her and were not able to make commitments.

A coworker invited Paula to our church group, where after a few months she decided to give God a chance. Filled with the sense of a fresh new beginning and the unexpected discovery that God really did love her after all, she decided to radically change her lifestyle and began looking for a Christian man with whom she could share her life and her new values.

But old habits die hard. In spite of new resolutions to be celibate, she soon found herself falling into sexual activity with Christian men. Actually, she admitted to partially seducing them. She wanted their attention and love, and sexual closeness had always been her way of securing those things. But even these new relationships with Christian men fell apart. Finally Paula met a wonderful man who had high moral standards, and a new, healthy relationship blossomed.

Now she had a new problem. She felt extremely guilty for the sexual sins of her past. Years of reckless sexuality weighed heavily on her soul. In her own words, she felt "dirty." She asked over and over for God's forgiveness, time and again for His cleansing. She knew intellectually that God forgave her. But she could not feel forgiven. Her head was clean, but her heart still felt dirty. She also felt unclean around her new fiancé. He had not been promiscuous. "He's clean and pure; and I'm not," she said. It was almost as if her soul had been stained.

This is the second and more tragic result of the sexual revolution in the lives of single adults. Years of sexual freedom not only cheapen people, but such behavior also taints them. Failure to live in sexual purity leaves the souls of singles filled with filth. The gospel promises forgiveness, but it is extremely difficult for such people to forgive themselves. It is even more difficult to feel forgiven by God.

TOUGH STAINS

The stain of sin sometimes penetrates deeply and is difficult to cleanse. Shakespeare, in his magnificent play *Macbeth*, gives us a vivid example of the difficulty in forgiving ourselves. After she and her husband ordered the murder of Banquo, Lady Macbeth washed the blood off her hands, but she could not wash the stain from her soul. Shakespeare portrays her as a tormented woman, experiencing terrifying nightmares. She imagines the blood is still on her hands, and she is unable to wash away the stain. A doctor is called to help her, and one night he and a servant observe her grisly sleepwalking actions:

Doctor: Hark! She speaks. I will set down what comes from her, to satisfy my remembrance the more strongly.

Lady M.: Out damned spot! Out, I say! One, two,—why, then it's time to do't. Hell is murky. Fie, my lord, fie! A soldier, and afeard? What need we fear who knows it, when none can call our power to account? Yet who would have thought the old man to have had so much blood in him?

Doctor: Do you mark that?

Lady M.: The Thane of Fine had a wife. Where is she now? What, will these hands ne'er be clean? No more o' that, my lord, no more o' that. You mar all with this starting.

. . .

Here's the smell of the blood still. All the perfumes of Arabia will not sweeten this little hand. Oh, oh, oh!

Doctor: What a sight is there! The heart is sorely charged.

Servant: I would not have such a heart in my bosom for the dignity of the whole body.

Lady Macbeth is dreaming, of course, that her hands are still stained with Banquo's blood, and no amount of washing can remove the stains. In her dreams she is walking with Macbeth, trying to wash her hands and convince him that Banquo cannot come back from the dead. She is thinking, *The power now is ours. Nothing can harm us.* Nothing can, except themselves and a slow destruction from inside. Lady Macbeth's heart was indeed "sorely charged," or heavily burdened. The burden would ultimately be the cause of her death. Not only was the stain unwashable, but in its filth was a poison that destroyed her soul.

Like the wise servant woman, none of us wants a heart filled with such pain. None of us could stand a soul loaded down with so much dirt.

This was Paula's problem. From her new perspective, the years of unclean living had produced a permanent stain. God might forgive her, but the feelings of being stained would remain. Even though the Bible said that God would forgive her sins and make her white as snow, she did not feel pure. She did not feel clean. If she were anything like snow, it was only trodden, muddy snow.

In a counseling session, her main question to me was honest: "How can I get rid of this feeling of uncleanliness? How can I get a sense of purity again?" Her question is common to many veterans of the sexual revolution, her need a common one in our generation.

The feelings of worthlessness and uncleanness are not restricted to one gender. Both men and women feel this way, in spite of the boastful language heard in locker rooms of both sexes. Both genders have suffered; both have been victimized. For Frank, Jerome, Phil, and Paula, the sexual revolution turned out to be a false promise, and, after following its instructions, they ended up worse than before.

If you are a weary victim of the sexual revolution and feel there's a stain you cannnot scrub clean, take heart. You can recover a feeling of value and worth again. Even singles who feel cheap and dirty can regain a sense of value and purity. Neither Phil nor Paula can wipe away the past; neither can you go back in time and undo poor choices. Fortunately, the Bible has a surprising and freeing solution, which we will discuss in the next chapter.

Questions for Discussion
1. In this section, consider the following people and how each would feel about his or her sexual value. Rate the person's sense of sexual worth, with 1 meaning no value and 7 meaning the person would feel great value.
   _____ (a) A thirty-five-year-old man who has never married, but has been sexually active.
   _____ (b) A thirty-five-year-old man who has never married and has been sexually inactive.
   _____ (c) A sixty-five-year-old woman who has recently lost her husband of forty years to death by cancer.
   _____ (d) A thirty-year-old divorcee with three small children and no college education.
   _____ (e) A twenty-three-year-old man who has been very active sexually and has begun to worry whether any of his former partners was infected with AIDS.
2. Think about your own sexual past. How do you think your past experiences may be influencing your present sexuality? Answer the following questions:
   (a) Do you remember past boyfriends/girlfriends and compare them to your current situation?
   (b) Do you have a hard time feeling pure and forgiven?
   (c) What things in your dating past do you regret and wish you could change?

3. In what other ways do you think the sexual revolution has influenced our culture? Can you think of both positive ways and negative ways?

4. Movies, TV, and novels are highly charged with sexual innuendoes and explicit content. How has popular media affected you, your attitude toward the opposite sex, and your current level of sexual satisfaction? How do you think the media's view of sexuality will affect you in the future?

5. This chapter suggests that the images we allow into our minds can cause us problems now and in the future. If this is true, how does this affect your lifestyle? Does it influence what TV shows you watch? The movies you see? The books or magazines you read? Why or why not?

CHAPTER FOUR

GOD'S SURPRISING ANSWER: THE VALUE OF SINGLE SEXUALITY

God has an answer to the question, "How can a person regain a sense of purity?" But fasten your seat belt—the answer is surprising and catches many singles off guard. In all the searching, many have not noticed the positive, transforming power of this solution. It is the ultimate stain remover. The answer is *temporary celibacy.*

The hidden, seldom understood value of celibacy is its purifying power. When celibate, a person withdraws from sexual activity for an extended period of time. This time apart is an opportunity; it is a harbor of rest and recovery. In this harbor, a single man can repair old damage and can find healing for past pains. A single woman can gain a whole new perspective on life and the place of sexuality. Temporary celibacy is a chance to recover a new sense of worth, and it is a season in which a new feeling of sexual purity can be discovered.

Those who have remained celibate may already know the benefits. Some feel the sense of purity and have strong feelings of self-worth. But most feel frustrated, even disappointed, that their sexual desires are not satisfied, and they don't feel a sense of wholeness. And for those singles who have had much sexual involvement and feel devalued, they can still restore their purity. They can return to wholeness. The solution is temporary celibacy, a celibacy that you continue to observe until your wedding day.

HIDDEN TREASURES

Kelly was a successful insurance agent, respected in the community and welcomed into our singles group. On the outside, he had it all together; but on the inside, he was a mess. He had made a lot of mistakes with women and as a result felt pretty worthless. One day I began a conversation with Kelly about home safes and how they protect our possessions. My purpose, of course, was to help him recognize the need to protect his sexual identity by staying celibate. The conversation began after Kelly made a confession to me.

"Rick, I'm a success in areas that really don't matter. But in the most important area—love—I'm a failure and a jerk."

I asked Kelly a simple question: "Do you have a safe or lock box in your home?"

Kelly replied, "Yes, I do."

"Well, where do you keep it? Is it usually on the kitchen table or the front porch?" I asked.

"Of course not," Kelly said. "It's kept hidden away in a safe place."

"Why do you hide it away? Are you embarrassed by it? Is it ugly or old or something?"

He said, "I hide it in a place where I think thieves won't look. I hide it to protect it."

"What do you keep in it—your dirty laundry or garden tools?"

With some sense of mounting exasperation, he responded, "No, I keep my valuables in there. Stuff like important documents, jewelry, keepsakes, and other valuable items."

"But if you keep your valuables hidden away, you and others can't enjoy them as often as if they were left out in the open. You're robbing yourself of pleasure!"

"That's true in one sense," Kelly said, "but in another sense if everyone could touch and handle my stuff, it would lose its value. Valuable things are sort of like rare coins. If everyone is allowed to hold a rare coin, not only might someone steal or lose it, but it will slowly wear away and will become less valuable. So if I don't keep my valuables locked up, I won't be able to enjoy them later because they will lose their value. I also collect baseball cards, but I don't let anyone handle them—that would cause them to lose value."

Kelly was on a roll now and just kept talking. "People also treat things better when they aren't left out in the open. If I bring a piece of crystal slowly out of a locked cabinet and gingerly give it to a friend to hold, he or she will treat it carefully. If I leave the same piece out on the coffee table, he or she might pick it up roughly, not knowing how valuable it is."

"Oh," I responded. "So locking something away is a way of asserting its worth. I bet I could put cheap stuff in a locked cabinet and people would assume it was really valuable."

"Sure." Kelly laughed. "That's an old interior decorator's trick!"

I summarized: "So you separate out the valuable stuff and hide it away, as a way of protecting and enhancing the items' value."

"That's right."

Kelly easily made the conclusion himself: Temporary celibacy ought to be viewed as an opportunity to withdraw from sexual activity in order to recover a sense of purity and worth.

THE VALUE OF VIRGINITY

Interestingly, a sense of purity and worth is exactly what the Bible conveys through the word *virgin*. The ancient Hebrews hid and separated the young women away as a way of protecting and asserting their worth. (The Hebrew words for "virgin" are made out of two roots meaning *to hide* and *to separate*.) It wasn't to hurt the women; it was to help them. It was a public declaration of their great value.

A brief word study is in order here. The Old Testament uses two Hebrew words for "virgin": *bethulah* and *almah*. *Bethulah* is the more common of the two in the Old Testament, occurring more than fifty times. When Abraham's trusted servant sought a bride for Abraham's son Isaac, he eventually saw Rebekah coming to the spring with a jar on her shoulder. "The girl was very beautiful, a virgin [*bethulah*]; no man had ever lain with her," according to Genesis 24:16. As Brown notes in *New International Dictionary of New Tesament Theology*, the word *bethulah* "always means an untouched maiden." Such a maiden was a source of hope for a suitor because he could be assured the offspring would be his, free from disease, and full of untapped potential.

Bethulah, therefore, metaphorically came to suggest the "embodiment of hope" and because of this was used as "a designation for the people of Israel"[1]

But *bethulah* meant much more than untouched, and the deeper significance of the word seems to have been missed by Becker and Brown. *Bethulah* was derived from an Arabic root meaning "to separate." It referred to someone who was separated from others and therefore not touchable. The Hebrew maidens were separated from the young men, removed from interaction. Of course, this was done not as a protection for the young men. It was the women who were being protected. Like fine jewels or expensive treasures, they were kept safe and secure from violation. Their separation was a way to protect their value; it was a clear statement to the community that a young woman was special and precious. Like a fine wine, she was not for everyone's use. She was being saved. She was special and unique.

This may be one reason why maidens in some Eastern countries wore (and still wear) veils to cover their faces. They were considered special, and that specialness was too valuable to let just anyone enjoy. The veils were a method of hiding away a treasure; the woman was being saved for one man. Letting any other man enjoy her beauty would be tantamount to her sharing her beauty with others, and the husband-to-be preferred to be the only one to enjoy his wife's loveliness. She was his precious treasure.

Of course, there were also other reasons that women wore veils—some of them not so positive, such as subordination, class status, and so on. But even when worn for negative reasons, the veils could have had a positive effect—guarding and protecting the value of the woman underneath.

This is similar to what happens today with attractive yet modest clothing. Though the clothes may reveal nothing, they nonetheless give the hint of what is underneath. Sometimes the hint is even more powerful that the real thing; a fully-clothed woman can look sexier than an unclad one. By wearing modest clothing, men and women can guard and protect the value underneath, while at the same time asserting that there is something of value there. This seems also to be the apostle Paul's point in 1 Corinthians 12:22–26: by clothing the unpresentable parts of the body, we give them "special treatment" and therefore "greater honor."

A similar root is behind the Hebrew word *almah*. The root *alm* simply meant *to hide*. It is used in Psalm 10:1, where the writer cries to God, "Why, O Lord, do you stand far off? Why do you hide [*almah*] yourself in times of trouble?"

Almah was also used to refer to young women who were of marriageable age or at least had not yet been married. In Genesis 24, Abraham's servant told of his discovery of Rebekah to her father Laban. He had referred to her in verse 16 as a virgin (*bethulah*), but this time he tells his story using the word *almah*:

> When I came to the spring today, I said, "O Lord, God of my master Abraham, if you will, please grant success to the journey on which I have come. See, I am standing beside this spring; if a maiden

[almah] comes out to draw water and I say to her, 'Please let me drink a little water from your jar,' and if she says to me 'Drink, and I'll draw water for your camels too,' let her be the one the Lord has chosen for my master's son." (vv. 42–43)

Almah is also the noun used in the famous passage in Isaiah 7:14, "Therefore the Lord Himself will give you a sign: The virgin [*almah*] will be with child and will give birth to a son, and will call him Immanuel."

The second Hebrew word for virgin, as we have seen, is constructed out of the word meaning "hidden." In other words, a virgin was "a hidden one," a young woman who was hidden away from others. This use is exactly parallel to the first Hebrew word for virgin, *bethulah,* which meant "separated one." In both cases, the central idea of virginity was to remove the woman from public access as a way of protecting and guaranteeing value. One did not separate, hide, and protect a worthless thing or person. Separation signified worth; hiding suggested value.

A RENEWED SENSE OF WORTH

A Hebrew virgin carried with her an inherent sense of value. When a virgin walked down the street, the observers would literally say in Hebrew, "Look, there goes a hidden one," or, "Say, there walks a separated one." A chaste (celibate) maiden knew that she was being saved. She had a tacit awareness that she was special and important. She was pure and therefore precious. To hear those words reinforced her own sense of specialness. They contributed to her deep sense of self-worth.

Unfortunately, the word *virgin* does not convey any sense of specialness or uniqueness today. A generation has passed since the late '60s when being a virgin was considered a sign of innocence, purity, and honor. Today many teenagers and adults consider *virgin* to be a negative word, implying a lack of worth, or immaturity. Young people ask one another, "You're not still a virgin, are you?" Even if they are, many teens will lie and say they are not. Being a virgin is not a mark of pride for youth today. Instead, it is a mark of failure, evidence that one is not pretty enough, grown up enough, or desirable. A virgin is one who hasn't scored yet, like a basketball player who can't make a basket.

How different it was for the young Hebrew women. They were valuable and special. The very words *bethulah* and *almah* were constant reminders of their worth. Maybe what we need to do is drop the English word *virgin* and start calling our young virgin teens *treasures* or *prizes.* Then they could say to anyone who wanted a cheap roll in the hay, "Forget it, Buster, I'm a treasure!" Like the Hebrew virgins of old, they would not only *be* pure, they would *feel* pure.

We also need new attitudes toward virginity, not just new words. Sadly, homosexuals today are free to come out of the closet, while virgins are forced into the closet! This needs to be changed. We need people who are proud of their purity. We need singles who are courageous about celibacy; and they, in turn, need friends who honor and support their virgin state—much like the *philoparthenos,* Christians in the fourth century who were called "lovers of virgins." We already have philosophers, philadelphians, and philantropists—what the world really lacks are philoparthenos.

IT'S GOTTA COST YOU SOMETHING

Purity had a price tag. A Hebrew maiden developed her sense of purity through years of separation. Probably many times the teenage girl wanted to run free, mingle with the other children, open the gates, throw off her veil, and flee from her hiding place. But she did not. Her sense of worth was established the old fashioned way—she earned it.

Even today, a sense of value and purity must be earned. After years of devalued living, a feeling of worth will take some time to develop. After years of thoughtless spending, it will take effort to build up a self-respect account again. Something this valuable and important cannot be had for free. Your decision to remain celibate—or to return to celibacy—will cost you. Ridicule, rejection for dates, perhaps even an ending to a relationship may await. You will face pressure to abandon this path.

Doing what is right sometimes requires such sacrifice. King David was aware of this principle. He serves as a remarkable model for single adults in the way he was willing to pay the price to achieve something worthwhile.

The second king of Israel, David led his armies to many grand victories. Eventually David began to feel prideful about his successes, and he decided to take a census of his troops. Joab, his commanding general, recognized this as a sinful thing to do and cautioned David against it. The king was beginning to rely on his human resources rather than on the Lord. Unfortunately, David took the census anyway.

In response to David's sin, God chose to punish Israel. Though David asked for the punishment to fall on him alone, God did not honor his request. Instead, God sent a plague in which thousands of Israelites died. God then asked David to go and build an altar on a certain spot of land, a threshing floor owned by Araunah the Jebusite. In obedience, David went to Araunah, and said to him: "Let me have the site of your threshing floor so I can build an altar to the Lord, that the plague on the people may be stopped. Sell it to me at the full price."

Araunah said to David, "Take it! Let my lord the king do whatever pleases him. Look, I will give the oxen for the burnt offerings, the threshing sledges for the wood, and the wheat for the grain offering. I will give all this" (1 Chronicles 21:22–23).

What a deal. David had been willing to pay for it, and here it was offered for free. Were I David, I would have been overjoyed. I probably would have thought, *How wonderful! Not only can I worship God, but Araunah can join in too. God probably had this whole thing planned out for us. He not only asked for an offering, but He arranged the payment.* I would have taken Araunah's offer, thinking that when God directs, He also supplies.

But David was not so shallow. He knew that an offering to God was not supposed to be free; it was supposed to cost something. That is why it was called a sacrifice. A free sacrifice is an oxymoron, a contradiction in terms. As the Scriptures report, "But King David replied to Araunah, 'No, I insist on paying the full price. I will not take for the Lord what is yours, or sacrifice a burnt offering that cost me nothing'" (v. 24).

This was a great principle—but how ironic that David did not practice this principle in the area of his sexuality. How different his life would have been if he had. Instead he enticed Bathsheba, the wife of one of his soldiers, to his palace. He lay with her, and she conceived a child. Later, compounding his lustful act, he had Bathsheba's husband placed on the front line of battle to die. The outcome of his actions was the death of one soldier, an illegitimate son, and turmoil in his kingdom.

A COSTLY PURITY AND A RECOVERED VIRGINITY

Sexual celibacy is the decision that sexuality is of value and personhood is special. When celibate, single adults are saying through their actions, "I will not reduce my sexuality to a cheap giveaway. I will not pretend it is unimportant or insignificant. It is valuable, and I am valuable. I will assert my worth and value by saving myself until marriage."

If the single adult at some later time in life meets another special single and decides to make a lifelong commitment, he/she then can say with pride: "Here, I give you my sexuality. It is pure again. I was not loose. I have saved myself. I am special and valuable. I give you my sexuality, but know this: This is not cheap. I am giving you something that cost me dearly. I am giving you something that no one has had—all of me. I would not stoop to offer you something that cost me nothing."

If the single chooses to remain unmarried, he or she still has a strong sense of personal worth and value. It is this sense of self-worth that brings contentment and fulfillment, not marital status. So whether a person marries or not, single celibacy is of great value. It's a win-win solution.

This is the wonder of celibacy, the opportunity that any single can grasp. Through asserting our worth and being mature enough to delay gratification, we can regain a sense of value that can last a lifetime or can someday be offered to another person with godly honor. Celibacy is a way of saying that we are special. It is a way to avoid reducing ourselves to a piece of worn-out luggage. By remaining celibate, we give physical testimony to the fact that our sexuality is a valuable treasure. We are not cheap, for we were bought for a price (1 Corinthians 6:20). In the same way, we will not give to someone that which cost us nothing, but only that for which we have paid the price.

One woman told me that understanding the value of her sexual identity and of staying sexually pure gave her the courage to tell men why she is staying celibate. "The fact that it is a valuable treasure and cost me a lot is so encouraging," she said. "I can place [that truth] before a man I am dating and say to him, 'This cost me a lot—I had to sacrifice a lot of relationships to give you this, so you better treat me well.' [My celibacy] enables me to think more highly of myself, and though I am thirty-six years old, to feel that I have something of value is a precious gift."

The price is temporary celibacy, but the prize is a deep sense of personal value and purity. Of course, one cannot recover a lost virginity in a technical, physical sense. There is no legalistic loophole, no way to turn back the hands of time. It is not like a lost coin that can be found, or a lost sheep that can be returned to the fold.

However, I would like to suggest that, theologically, virginity *can* be recovered. As the Scriptures proclaim, when God forgives us, our sins are wiped out and forgotten. The grace of God is able to turn the blackest of sins "as white as snow" (Isaiah 1:18). I often tell this to remarried couples, as well as to singles who have been sexually promiscuous in the past. God is really good at forgiving, and the Scriptures do not say that God will only cleanse you as white as a *peach*. In His eyes you are pure, and because of that you are free to wear white on your wedding day. In a spiritual sense, you have recovered your virginity; God sees your sins as fully cleansed, turned white as snow.

But can such a sense of purity be recovered in an emotional, personal way? This was the question that began this chapter and the question that burned in Paula's heart. It is the question that torments many singles. "I know that God has forgiven me, but how can I forgive myself? How can I feel forgiven? How can I feel pure again?"

The answer is temporary celibacy. People who desire to regain a sense of purity and value need to take some time apart; they need to hide themselves sexually. They must go through the Hebrew process of asserting worth by removing the valuable object. They need to be celibate for a while in order to feel like a virgin again. To see the joy of celibacy and the power to restore one's value, read "A Single Speaks."

A SINGLE SPEAKS

Ninth grade was really the big year for me. At Christmastime in the youth group I met a boy that I really liked, and I could tell he liked me. He was 17 (a senior), and I was 14 (a freshman). We went out in groups first for about four months. Then we finally went on an official date. I was so scared! He had tried to kiss me before, but I would turn my head. So on this date, he finally kissed me. I was excited and scared all at the same time. That began a relationship that lasted one and one-half years. Over the first year, kissing progressed to touching to oral sex . . . and finally to intercourse.

He told me it was OK to have sex if you were going to get married. He also said you were still a virgin if you didn't have intercourse. I didn't really believe the part about intercourse. I figured if you were having oral sex, you were having sex—but I justified it because I believed with all my heart that we would marry, and I loved him very much.

By the time of my junior year, things were getting old. I wanted to be a high schooler; he wanted to be in college. So we broke up. I wanted to break up, but I felt so much guilt over it because now we weren't going to get married. I felt like I had sinned. . . .

As time went on and more relationships ensued, sex was nearly always a part of it. That first relationship seemed further and further away. I viewed it as a time of innocence and youthfulness. By the time I was 19, I felt old and weathered. I hated men. I was bitter, a hardened shell. I attributed my state of mind to betrayal. The men in my life had betrayed me. I felt like a victim, and my retaliation was bitterness and hatred. By that time, I had slept with probably ten different men, some of whom I can't even remember any more.

At this point, Christ rescued me. My first boyfriend got in touch with me again. I turned my life over to Christ, and we began to date again. He wanted to remain abstinent, but I didn't understand why (sex with him was a good thing). But I followed his lead, and my ideas changed over time. I think God gave me a new virginity.

My bitterness toward men slowly dissipated. We married two years later. God has restored me. However, I still have those memories of the past that I try to forget because I am ashamed of my behavior. I had no idea I was selling myself cheaply. I just felt like a victim of circumstances. My own lack of self-esteem was directly related to my lack of sexual control. I desperately wanted to be loved and cared for. I never really felt loved for myself, except by my husband. I'm just so glad God pulled me up and gave me a new start.

HOW TEMPORARY IS CELIBACY?

Note carefully that, since most singles eventually will marry, celibacy is only *for a while*. I am not advocating that singles take a vow of celibacy as a permanent, lifelong lifestyle. We are not hoping to establish a new order of evangelical monasteries and convents. As Jesus well knew, very few persons were called to be celibate for a lifetime. Only those few are called to a permanent celibacy. But all singles are called to a *temporary celibacy*. This is not a lifelong, eternal vow. It is a temporary decision to withdraw from sexual activity as a way of regaining a sense of personal worth and purity.

Temporary celibacy begins with a decision. If a single adult wanted to be active sexually but couldn't find a date for six months, this would not constitute what I am calling temporary celibacy. One cannot be intentionally celibate by default. Though such a person has been without sex for a while, he/she hasn't been celibate mentally. Instead, he has been active mentally, working at the game. If a hunter has been on a deer hunt but was unsuccessful, we still refer to him as a hunter. Just because he has not fired a shot does not mean he is an animal-rights activist. In the same way, it takes more than a stretch of what a sexual hunter might call "bad luck" to call one celibate. It takes a personal and voluntary decision.

CAN ONLY WOMEN BE VIRGINS?

From our earlier discussion of the Hebrew words for "virgin," you may conclude that biblical virginity applies only to women and that women are saddled with both the responsibility to assert their value and the sacrifice in order to protect it. I didn't correct this mistaken assumption at some of my early seminars and received several reminders as a result.

One woman wrote, "This system of separating the girls seems to be unfair to the girls. Why not expect the same accountability from the boys? Are boys better? More valuable to God? Why not expect the same sacrifices from boys!" Another woman called the seminar "sexist" and offered this concise response: "My main suggestion to improve the seminar is: Don't look at this issue as putting the burden of chastity on women."

This perception was quite puzzling to me—I had consciously tried to present a balanced view. I was quite careful to balance the stories, so that men and women were both represented. My language was not sexist. So I looked deeply at the implications of my statements about women/maidens guarding themselves as treasures.

The problem, I think, came in dealing with the Old Testament and its view of gender and sexual relations. Anyone who reads the Old Testament today will notice its pronounced patriarchal emphasis. It is not news that the Hebrew culture described in the Old Testament Scriptures was very sexist. The male leaders of family units held the vast majority of the rights, and women were regarded as possessions of these male leaders. Husbands, for instance, were able to divorce their wives, whereas most wives had no such privilege. Polygamy by men was the accepted norm; polygamy by women (technically called polyandry) was not allowed. Only males could serve as priests, and only men could enter the inner court of the temple. When the census was taken, only men of fighting age (twenty years old and above) were counted. In these and numerous other ways, women were victims of discrimination.

However, the women did not often object to this system. In the highly nomadic and difficult life led by those ancient peoples, the patriarchal system provided a stable and workable social structure that is difficult for us to understand.

The harsh reality of life precluded anyone's being able to survive alone; an extended family or clan was necessary for survival. There were no grocery stores, clothing outlets, nursing homes, or hospitals. Every need—especially food, clothing, and shelter—had to be provided by the family or tribe. Because of this, neither single men nor single women could have survived alone. Because strength and power meant survival during this period of savagery and warfare, a tribe could survive only if it were capable of protecting itself. A weak tribe did not survive, except as slaves. Because of these and many other factors, patriarchalism was the cultural norm that existed during this era.

The Mosaic law did not critique this deeply embedded system of male dominance but instead showed how any authority had to submit to an even higher authority—that of God. (This is similar to the way the New Testament did not critique the social system of slavery; to do so would have deprived many slaves of the ability to make a living. Instead, masters were told to submit to a higher authority, the Lord Jesus.) Even though the Mosaic law did not critique a social system, that does not imply approval. In fact, a good argument can be made that the New Testament corrects this misunderstanding; in Christ, both males and females are equal (Galatians 3:28).

So how are we to view the social system in regard to virginity? Since only young women had to separate and hide themselves in the Hebrew culture, are we to conclude that the responsibility for sexual purity today rests mainly on the women? Or can we extend the benefits of hiding and separating to the male sex?

Clearly, it makes no sense to restrict virginity to females, because that would suggest that only women develop their sense of self-worth through how they are treated physically. As we have seen, men also feel devalued and contaminated when celibacy outside of marriage is abandoned. Men also can recover their sense of personal and physical worth through a period of extended, temporary celibacy. So the advantages of celibacy apply equally to both sexes, even though in the Old Testament these advantages were enjoyed only by the women.

Both single men and single women are valuable, and their value is best protected and asserted by celibacy. And in order to feel valuable and grow to appreciate their own worth, both sexes need to pay a price, both need to sacrifice, both need to remain celibate until marriage.

Today, the value of virginity can apply equally to both sexes. Both men and women are privileged to be able to recover a sense of worth and purity, what some people are calling today a *secondary virginity*. But for me, there is nothing secondary about it. In God's eyes, if you are pure, then you are pure.

It doesn't matter whether you are pure because you have been well-hidden or because you have been well-forgiven. God forgives and makes sin "as white as snow." The feeling of purity and worthiness before God is an experience available to both male and female singles, with equal costs and equal benefits.

A HAPPY ENDING

I am happy to say that Paula was able to achieve a happy ending. She made a decision to change her lifestyle of sexual involvement with others, to separate herself. It was, of course, a very difficult thing to do. At times she felt unloved and unwanted. She often felt out of control and helpless. But in time, she began to feel a sense of pride in herself again and a sense of spiritual cleanliness. By voluntarily abstaining from sexual activity for a time, she regained a sense of purity.

In her own words, "I always felt that celibacy meant being unlovely and unwanted. The last thing on my mind was to do without sexual involvement with men. So I went to bed with them, but I'd wake up feeling cheap anyway!

"After trying everything else, my eyes were finally opened to the real value of celibacy. I've been celibate for a year now, and I feel great. I am proud of myself! I'm not a floozy anymore. I'm someone special!

"I've also fallen in love with a man and haven't slept with him! That's a big change for me. We are very sexually attracted to one another, but we still keep to our standards. And you know, I know it sounds crazy, but I feel more sexual with him than I have with any other man! It's like the celibacy makes us appreciate one another more.

"In addition to that, I feel pure with him. I know this is a relationship that is honoring God and is building on the right foundations. Bill loves me for the person I am, not just for a sex partner. And he's lucky to have me—I'm a valuable woman again! And if our relationship continues to grow and we decide to marry, I've decided to wear a white wedding dress. Just like you always say, Rick—God doesn't forgive our sins as white as peach!"

Many singles have made discoveries just like Paula. Through temporary celibacy, they have discovered a new sense of worth. Through abstinence, they have found a new feeling of purity. These men and women are proud of themselves too, and they have reason to be. They were wise enough to take advantage of one of God's more surprising opportunities. They discovered themselves, and now they have something positive to give to someone else if they choose.

Celibacy is an opportunity that God offers to all single adults. It is a harbor of recovery and renewal, a place where value can be found. It is a harbor that Paula and many others have navigated successfully. Remember, a voluntary period of sexual abstinence will let you set yourself aside and regain a sense of value and self-worth. It will let you develop a new feeling of purity. It is a gift of God, a blessing in disguise. These are the advantages to temporary celibacy, and together they make up the positive side of single sexuality—the positive reason why singles can *desire* to be temporarily celibate until marriage.

Hannah was a lovely, sixty-five-year-old single woman who had the desire to remain celibate until marriage, but she had two boyfriends, each pressuring her to go to bed with them. She struggled with the relationships for some time, thinking that maybe she was being old-fashioned. When she discovered that her celibacy was a way of protecting and asserting her worth, she found the strength to confront these men. I'll always remember and treasure what she told me, as she took my arm, led me to a corner of the room, and whispered to me.

"Rick, remember that conversation we had about my two boy-friends who were pressuring me sexually? Well, I finally broke up with both of them!"

"What?" I whispered back. "I thought you liked them?"

"I did," she said. "But I realized that if they were pressuring me to go to bed, they didn't really value me for who I was and what I wanted. So I told them both, 'Hey, I'm a million dollar table! I'm not going to let you scratch my surface anymore!'"

Questions for Discussion

1. Do you agree or disagree with this idea of celibacy and its relationship to sexual worth? Why? 2. How long would one need to be celibate in order to feel pure again?

3. In what other areas besides sexuality might it be wise for singles to be celibate for a time?

4. Do you agree with the concept that sacrifice is offering to God something that cost us something? _____ Why? If this is so, how will it affect our relationship to God in areas other than sexuality?

5. Read 2 Corinthians 11:2 and Revelation 14:4. What do these passages add to the concept of celibacy?

PART TWO

WHY DOES GOD LEAVE OUR SEX SWITCHES ON?

CHAPTER FIVE

DOES SEX GUARANTEE INTIMACY?

Because they lack a positive reason for their single sexuality, many singles feel only frustration, temptation, and confusion. Single sexuality is seen as an unmanageable subject, an unprofitable problem. The only solution is to avoid anything to do with sexuality. Such singles end up looking like the "see no evil, hear no evil, speak no evil" monkeys. Of course, a life of avoidance is very difficult for singles: they are to see no sex, hear no sex, speak no sex, and touch no sex. That's an impossibility; there's no way to become a nonsexual person.

An overweight woman complained one day, "It's easier to be an alcoholic than an overeater. At least the alcoholics can live without booze, and they can avoid their problem completely. But we can't live without food. We have to face our problem every day, to taste and be tempted, and yet not give in. Can you imagine an alcoholic staying sober if he was forced to drink some wine with every meal?" In the same way, singles try to keep away from sexual reminders, but in our sexually hyper-charged culture they are constantly bombarded with the very thing they are trying to avoid.

Laura, for instance, was an intelligent, conservative Christian, and a virgin. She was sexually pure and innocent, trying to save herself for her future husband. She felt the virgin lifestyle was difficult in her late teens, as she was quite popular and dated frequently. But she kept to her standards. Her romantic life took a few unexpected turns, and she graduated from college unmarried. She was again successful and popular in the working world, but few of the men she met were Christians. She dated some of her co-workers, staunchly retaining her moral ideals. Though they made many sexual advances, she withstood them all.

When Laura reached her twenty-fifth birthday, though, she began to become depressed about her marital potential. All of her friends had already married, as had all of the quality Christian men she knew. She was a virgin, indeed, and despaired of ever being married.

"Why do all of my friends get to be sexual and I do not?" She asked. "If God wants me to remain single, then why did He create me as a woman with the desires I have? I want to experience physical intimacy with a man too! I feel as if God made a mistake or just forgot about me. Sometimes I even think he is just playing with me, getting some morbid satisfaction out of my pain. That's not the way I used to view God—and not the way I want to view Him—but sometimes I can't help it."

It was all just too confusing to her. Why did God leave all of her sexual apparatus in full functioning order and yet hang a sign on it that said, "Do not use"? Why did she have all of this equipment and no freedom to use it? Why was she barred from the experiences of closeness and physical intimacy?

She asked these questions of many Christian leaders and friends. They gave her answers, many of them simplistic and trite. They all seemed merely to say, "Because God said no." None was able to sufficiently explain to her *why* He said no.

Finally, Laura made up her own mind. She decided to become sexually active. Her decision process went something like this: *God is loving and smart. He doesn't make mistakes, and He is not malicious. He created me as a sexual woman. I am going to experience all that He created me to be.*

This new type of sexual freedom was exhilarating for Laura, but it also brought with it a truckload of new problems. Even though she was being more physical with men, she felt even further from them. Somehow the sexual behavior was preventing the development of closeness. The men stopped treating her with consideration; they were less interested in expensive evenings out on the town. In addition, her self-esteem began to plummet, as she realized men wanted her for sex—not for her many fine character qualities. Finally, her relationship with God diminished considerably, as did her involvement in church and with Christian friends.

Laura was not happy or content. Even more terrible was the realization that she was not any closer to becoming what she was created to be. She was at last sexually active, but she lost her self-esteem.

ARE MANY CHRISTIAN SINGLES SEXUALLY ACTIVE?

Laura is not the only single Christian who has decided to become sexually active. If the studies and surveys are correct, Laura is part of the majority, not the minority. In order to understand how many Christian singles are sexually active, it is important to first look at the larger context of sexual activity of all singles. Many studies have been done along these lines, all of them drawing the same conclusions: most singles are sexually active and are confused about moral issues. Reay Tannahill, in her encyclopedic work *Sex in History,* refers to a study done by *Time* magazine that illustrates this well:

> A swift result of the 1970s" sexual revolution was moral confusion. When *Time* magazine conducted a survey toward the end of 1977, it found that 61 percent of the people interviewed were finding it "harder and harder to know what"s right and what"s wrong these days." In the 35 to 49 age group, 72 percent thought it was "morally wrong" for teenagers to have sexual relations; among the over-fifties the figure rose to 80 percent. Forty-two percent of those questioned believed women should be virgins at marriage, and 34 percent that men should be, too. (There was an apparent conflict here between theory and practice, since a survey, a year earlier, had indicated that at least 55 percent of unmarried women and 85 percent of men had had intercourse by the age of 19.) Forty-seven percent still considered homosexuality "morally wrong," 43 percent did not, and 10 percent were unsure. Yet although 74 percent wanted the government to crack down on pornography in movies, book, and nightclubs, 70 percent subscribed to the statement that "there should be no laws, federal or state, regulating sexual practice." Men on the whole tended to be more liberal than women, Catholics more permissive than Protestants. [1]

The trend to sexual permissiveness has now reached the general teenage population. A nationwide survey conducted in 1992 by the Centers for Disease Control in Atlanta polled 11,631 students in grades nine to twelve and found these results: 40 percent of ninth graders claim to have had sex, 58 percent of tenth graders, 57 percent of eleventh graders, and a whopping 72 percent by time they are seniors.

Things have changed rapidly over the past forty years. In 1948 the Kinsey Report stated that 80 percent of all American men under the age of 25 admitted to some premarital, sexual experience. In 1953, Kinsey reported that 33 percent of women under age 25 were in some way sexually active (either there were some busy women or some men and women who lied!) But by 1975, *Redbook* magazine asked its female readers a similar question. It reported that 90 percent of the women under age 25 admitted to being sexually active. The sexual revolution had obviously made an impact on the behavior of young women.

The *Redbook* survey, however, also asked a significant religious question of its readers. It asked them to classify the strength of their religious commitment. Of the women under age 25 who claimed to be strongly religious, 75 percent still admitted to sexual experience before marriage. [2]

A 1987 Barna survey conducted for Josh McDowell Ministry found a majority of Christian teenagers to be sexually active. Polling more than 1,400 youth who attend church, Barna found that by age eighteen 65 percent had had sexual contact, ranging from fondling to intercourse, and 43 percent had engaged in sexual intercourse. Interestingly, 73 percent of the youth who said they had experienced sexual intercourse said they were born-again Christians. [3]

Why are so many strongly religious singles sexually active? Maybe one of the reasons lies in the instructions on sexual morals that their churches are giving. In order to determine the theological and moral beliefs of church leaders in America, researchers William McKinney and Daniel Olson in 1988 and 1989 distributed 3,000 questionnaires to national leaders of several denominations, ranging from the United Church of Christ to the Assemblies of God. Of almost 1,500 denominational leaders who responded, only 40 percent felt it was wrong for a man and a woman to have sexual relations before marriage. Of course, the specific denominational percentages varied widely: of the United Church of Christ, only 14 percent of its leadership believed premarital sexual relations to be wrong, contrasting with 95 percent of the Assembly of God leaders who felt such activity was wrong. The percentages of leaders in other denominations that felt premarital sexual activity was wrong were: United Methodist Church, 36 percent; American Baptist Churches, 45 percent; Baptist General Conference, 95 percent; Evangelical Free Church, 94 percent; and the governing board members and national staff of the National Council of Churches, 19 percent. [4]

Obviously, opinions among Protestant church leadership vary widely as to whether sexual activity before marriage is wrong. No wonder so many Christian single adults become sexually involved; the messages they hear from church leaders are mixed and confusing, to say the least. Even in the most conservative denominations, there are leaders who do not believe premarital sexual activity to be wrong. In the more liberal churches, there are leaders who openly model unmarried, sexually active lifestyles.

Clearly Laura is not alone; many single adults, even Christian single adults, are sexually active today. All are missing the hidden opportunities God has for single adults in temporary celibacy. Typically, they have ignored the option of celibacy, associating it only with traditional morality, not even considering its emotional and spiritual benefits. Contrary to the common sense adage "Don't throw the baby out with the bathwater," our culture has jettisoned not only traditional morality, but also the practical benefits of temporary celibacy.

TRYING TO SAIL WITHOUT A RUDDER

We are a culture adrift without any guidelines for sexual behavior or morals. "We've thrown out the old values that inhibited sexuality and we can't agree on the new ones," says Richard J. Cross, professor emeritus at the Rutgers University School of Medicine. "The task is now to try and agree on what constitutes mutual responsibility in a relationship." Coss, an academic, affirms what the Bible has been saying all along, that standards are needed for our sexual behavior.

However, the professionals can't agree, Cross says. How confusing, then, it must be for the average person. As Richard Keeling, chairman of the American College Health Task Force on AIDS, says, "There's a great sense of chaos now when young people consider sexual activity. Students frequently tell you in confidential interviews that the risks they perceive far outweigh the pleasures of sex." However, "There's still a pattern of one-night stands and numerous partners," according to June Reinisch, director of the Kinsey Institute for Sex Research. In fact, research shows that 90 percent of young women today have had intercourse before marriage, compared with only 60 percent forty years ago. [5]

Recently, a TV station in southern California broadcast the tragic news of a local high school baseball player who shot himself in the head during the bus ride home after a game. He and some fellow athletes were playing Russian roulette with a loaded pistol, and he lost. Noting that his accidental suicide was a needless loss of life and the result of a senseless risk, the evening news anchors cautioned other teens against playing that stupid game.

Yet TV news anchors fail to warn young people against playing another form of Russian roulette played by millions of the nation's teens and adults. Sexual Russian roulette is just as devastating, for it can lead to contact with the deadly Human Immunodeficency Virus (HIV). How wonderful it would be to hear some of the TV anchors say, "Premarital sexual activity is a dangerous game in which there are no winners, only the potential of a needless loss of life because of a stupid game." But of course, they don't say this, because they think abstinence is impossibly hard for young singles. That's nonsense.

After basketball star Magic Johnson admitted to the world that he had been tested as HIV positive, it became clear that such extramarital and premarital sexual behavior, in light of the current AIDS epidemic, was very risky. He had played a sexual form of Russian roulette. Though he thought himself invincible, he too succumbed to the disease. Originally Johnson told teens to practice "safe sex" to avoid getting HIV. Now he recognizes that the only safe sex is no sex at all, and Johnson teaches abstinence to avoid getting AIDS.

Yet the modern media mainly teach the simple (and potentially deadly) slogan "Practice Safe Sex." That's like saying to teens, "It's OK to play Russian roulette as long as you wear a helmet." What dumb advice. What if the helmet has a crack or weak spot? If we truly believe kids can say no to drugs, what prevents us from believing that kids can successfully say no to sex before marriage? We assume they can't, though, and offer them condoms and warnings to encourage them on their way.

In fact, drug education in the classroom is a useful analogy that illustrates how mixed up the ethics of sex education are today. Can anyone imagine a science teacher's giving a lecture like this:

"OK, class, today we will learn about drug abuse. Now of course you shouldn't take drugs unless prescribed by a physician. But we educators know that that is an old fashioned belief and that most of you will take drugs anyway. So today we want to show you the healthy way to do cocaine, heroin, and many other drugs. Let's start with heroin. First, it's really important that you use a clean needle. After class, I will be giving out free needles to anyone who wants one. Next, you roll up your sleeve, make a fist, and . . ."

This, of course, is easily seen as a counterproductive way to teach drug prevention. Unfortunately, the very same method in the area of sexuality is seen as "enlightened" and "modern."

A PROBLEM FOR THOSE
PREVIOUSLY MARRIED TOO

The problem of a strong sex drive and the temptation for sex before marriage does not confront only young singles. In fact, the problem may be even more difficult for those singles who have been previously married. It is extremely difficult for some singles to be sexually active for several years and then to become completely inactive. It's like asking a marathon runner never to jog again, an artist never to paint, a chef never to eat. If sexual activity has become a vital part of a person's life and identity, it is confusing and painful to quench that behavior.

Alan was a happily married man of forty-five with three children and a loving wife. Driving home one night from a meeting, his wife lost control of her car and drove into a tree. She was killed on impact. Alan's world, of course, turned instantly upside down. He was now both father and mother, breadwinner and homemaker. Friends and family helped out in many ways, and he and his children slowly rebuilt their lives.

But no one helped Alan with his sexual problem. He had been sexually active with his wife for years. After his wife's death, he was expected instantly to change and become celibate. As he said, "Do you have any idea how hard it is to be sexually active one day, and then the next day to be celibate? Lots of things about June's death were difficult, but at least others could help. No one helped me sexually—no one even mentioned a word! And I couldn't talk to anyone about it. I was embarrassed. It's still a tough problem for me!"

Divorced singles often feel the same way. As Tracy, a single woman divorced at thirty-one, put it: "Alex and I were a terrible match in every way but sexually. It may sound sick, but sex basically kept our marriage together for as long as it lasted. In bed we were great; out of bed, we were rotten.

"We finally realized that most of life is lived out of bed! We knew the best thing for both of us was the divorce, and I don't regret it. But I was surprised to find out how hard it was to be celibate. After eleven years of great sex, I was going crazy after eleven days. Of course, I couldn't talk about it with my married Christian friends—they already looked down on me for getting the divorce. This is the first time I've ever admitted to anyone how hard it was to not be sexually active."

Tracy met a man and married him three months after her divorce was final. You probably can guess one of the reasons that drove her to marry again so quickly. Unfortunately, the second marriage also did not work out. Tracy is now trying to take things slowly and not jump into a new relationship right away, but she admits that it still is difficult. "I feel such a desire to share intimacy with a man that I give in sometimes. Is that so wrong?"

"PLEASE GOD, TURN OFF MY SWITCH!"

Of course, not all singles are sexually active. There are still many who are virgins, trying hard to remain pure. These singles are not sexually active, yet many of them feel as Laura and Tracy do: they too are frustrated and confused. Why does God make them sexual and then prohibit sexual activity?

In desperation, many singles turn to God as the final solution. They cry to God for release from their sexual feelings. They envision God standing before a great, heavenly control panel, able to turn on and off the different impulses in their lives. So they beg God to turn off their sex switch.

"How nice it would be," they assume, "if God would just turn us off sexually while we are single. We could then be without these strong temptations for a while and be better able to lead godly lives. Of course, God could flip my switch back on once I become married. What a great idea."

I have often wondered what marriage ceremonies would be like if singles were granted this wish. As the pastor pronounced the couple married, or as the two exchanged vows, God in heaven would move their sex switches from OFF to ON. How funny that would be to watch. I can see single men and women, having had no sexual impulses for months or years, begin to quiver and shake as these impulses coursed through their veins again. (Some might even faint from systems overload.) Their eyes would become like saucers, the first kiss would be much more passionate, and the recessional would be very fast. In fact, receptions after weddings might become a thing of the past.

But God, for reasons of His own, does not choose to answer this prayer as some singles have hoped. Instead, He leaves singles' sex switches fully on and functioning.

Singles who are not having sexual activity aren't sure why God has left them so turned on (literally), and because of this they aren't sure why they are still waiting. As one single woman said, "I know single Christians aren't supposed to be sexual, but I've almost had enough of this waiting. I'm about to give in anyway!"

INTIMACY AND THE SUPER SEX MYTH

The reason for the large numbers of sexually active singles is not primarily physical. Unlike those lines in the movies and in real life, men won't explode if they don't get sex. For most men and women, the physical sex drive is not so overwhelming that we will go crazy if we don't get release.

The body has its own mechanisms for releasing such sexual pressure. A man may say to a woman, "Please make love to me. If we don't, I think I'll explode." But she should be wiser than that and have more of a sense of self-respect than to make love just to be a human release valve. One smart woman told me that she just said to one such man, "Sorry, but that's just another reason I shouldn't sleep with you."

No, the motivating factor towards sexual involvement for singles is not primarily physical. Instead, it is *relational*. The top priority for single adults is their hunger for close, personal relationships. What we really want is *intimacy*. We need closeness with another human being, a sense of being cherished by one special individual. Intimacy is the draw.

But what does this have to do with sexual behavior? The connection is easy, at least in twentieth-century America. It is expressed by what we might call "The Super Sex Myth" of our culture: sex will guarantee intimacy.

There is, of course, some truth to this myth, as there is in all mythic beliefs. An emotion similar to intimacy is felt when clothing is removed, and each person reveals what is kept from public view. A feeling of closeness is sometimes experienced when two people lie down side by side, touching and being touched. A sense of being cherished is approximated by the intensity with which the two cling to one another, holding each other tightly.

But the myth is ultimately false. Sex does not necessarily provide intimacy. Instead, it can prevent true intimacy from ever occurring, genuine vulnerability from happening, authentic closeness from being achieved. In the wrong context, sex can be the enemy of intimacy.

ACCEPT NO SUBSTITUTES

And yet the myth continues. Singles may substitute sexuality for intimacy out of ignorance, or they may actually settle for sexuality instead of seeking intimacy. Here are three reasons singles may be tempted to substitute sexuality for intimacy:

First, sex is easier than honesty. Sex is less risky than true vulnerability. Most of us find it very difficult to openly reveal ourselves to another person—especially if we don't know for sure who we are. So we hide behind our passion, and we hide together under the sheets.

This is one reason teenagers are notorious for kissing for hours— kissing is easier than talking. The process of forming themselves, their ideas, and their goals is just beginning. How can they talk with any depth? Even more difficult is the sharing of emotions. Emotions are still hard to identify and express. So how can they truly share verbally what they are feeling? These tasks are too demanding for teenagers; indeed, they are tough even for adults. Rather than attempt to scale their heights, the kids opt instead for a satisfying and yet easily accessible plateau: lookout point.

Frequently the same inability to share a true sense of self with another persists into adulthood. Maybe the man has a very poor sense of self, so it is better kept hidden. Maybe the woman was deeply hurt before, so she keeps her real self hidden and protected as a way of avoiding future pain. Whatever the cause, these adults are likely to choose sex over intimacy. They take the clothes off their bodies but keep the masks on their faces. Intimacy has degenerated into a costume party, each playing a tightly scripted part. Such behavior reminds me of a masquerade ball at a nudist colony. Neither knows who the other really is.

This has happened partly because of laziness; it takes a lot of work to know and be known. But it also has occurred because of fear. Discovering the true essence of another person is a dangerous thing, as is being truly known. If I do not know the real you, then I can continue to believe that you are who I would like you to be. But if I know the real you, I'm stuck with that. My ability to idealize you is over.

In the same way, if you do not know the real me, it won't hurt so much if you reject me. After all, that really wasn't me you rejected. But if you truly know me and still reject me, the pain is complete and deep. As John Powell said in *Why Am I Afraid to Tell You Who I Am?* "If I tell you who I am, you may not like who I am, and that is all I have."

Second, sex can be a quick fix. In a world of microwave ovens and Minute-Rice®, the ability to delay gratification is hindered, if not completely absent. Not only are our children unable to sit quietly and politely, and not only are our teenagers unable to do their chores or homework first and relax later, but we adults are also largely unable to delay gratification. Rather than waiting to save enough money to buy more clothes, our credit cards are loaded to the limit. Rather than investing in the safe, long-term account, our money is lost in high-risk, get-rich-quick investments. And rather than waiting until commitments are made and we know that the person is able and willing to keep the commitment, we jump into bed hoping that commitments will follow.

Scott Peck, author of *The Road Less Traveled,* says that "delaying gratification is the process of scheduling the pain and pleasure of life in such a way as to enhance the pleasure by meeting and experiencing the pain first and getting it over with." He claims, "It is the only decent way to live."[6] The quick-fix approach to sexuality is the opposite of decent, mature sexuality that can endure delayed gratification. Like a drug, it only masks the need and numbs the feelings. Prolonged use of this drug can lead to an addiction, an addiction to shallowness and dishonesty. It leaves one with neither a decent nor a gratified life.

Third, sex even can be used as an avoidance of intimacy. Two singles who have just met at a bar and later hop into bed may be intimate physically, but there is little potential for emotional or relational intimacy. Sometimes they don't even know each other's names. The greatest example of such avoidance can be seen in what are known today as fake orgasms. At the height of what should be an honest, vulnerable moment, there yet can be extreme falsehood and dishonesty. Rather than intimacy, one partner will lie to the other about the very physical act that is supposedly going on. Here there is not even physical intimacy anymore; there is only theater. Modern singles have effectively replaced the desire for intimacy with the deceit of imitation.

Deep down we know that sex does not guarantee intimacy. Women still roll over in bed and ask their men, "Do you love me?" The men answer back with an annoyed sound, "Of course, I love you. We just had sex, didn't we?" But both the woman and the man know better: sex does not guarantee intimacy, and sometimes it is used to avoid it. As any married couple knows, the marriage bed can be the loneliest place on earth.

Sex not only doesn't guarantee intimacy, but it can also destroy it. If that is the case, then why does God leave singles' sex switches on? The surprising answer will be revealed in the next two chapters.

Questions for Discussion
1. Did you ever wish that God would unplug your sex drive? When? Why?
2. Did you ever wish that God would unplug someone else's sex drive? When and why?
3. If Laura had come to you with her story as a frustrated virgin, what would you have said to her? Why?

4. If singles avoid or repress their sexual urges, that energy will probably come out in some other way—usually destructive. What ways
   do you think that repressed sexuality affects singles? Give some
   concrete examples of things that singles do that may be an unconscious result of their avoided sexuality.
5. Are you surprised at the beliefs about premarital sexuality by the
   denominational leaders? Why or why not?
6. Do you think the comparison with Russian roulette is an apt one?
   Can you think of any other dangerous games that we could compare
   active single sexuality with?
7. Do you agree with the three main reasons that singles still try to
   substitute sexuality for intimacy? Why or why not? Can you think of
   any other reasons that singles might choose to substitute sexuality
   for intimacy?

CHAPTER SIX

WHY DID GOD MAKE US MALE AND FEMALE?

Paul is a forty-something, successful minister in a mid-sized, affluent church. He is respected as a loving shepherd, a devoted father and husband, and a community leader. By outside appearances, one would assume that Paul deals well with his sexuality. He avoids coarse jokes, preaches against R-rated movies, and has remained faithful to his wife. But on the inside, Paul has struggled for many years with his sexuality, and his past still haunts him. Much of it traces to his rearing at home and church. Let's listen in as he tells his story:

> I was born in the late forties and raised to believe that sex was not something to be discussed. It was a forbidden subject at home and at church. I attended a conservative Christian college in the Midwest where again there was no discussion of sexual issues or sexual problems. They were "sinful," and if you were "right with God," you wouldn't have those types of problems. The college was fearful that students might have sex, that a girl would become pregnant, and the school would lose its support from [that girl's home] church. The concern was so great that even the cafeteria was divided down the middle—there was the boys' side and the girls' side. There was no sitting together even for dinner. You could go out on a date from 7:00–11:00 P.M. on Friday and between church services on Sunday—that was it!
>
> In that environment I learned that sex was not a subject to be discussed. If you ignored it, then you wouldn't have a problem in

the church. In spite of this, it became a great problem for me, personally and professionally. It took me many years to learn to counsel people without being embarrassed when sex was brought up as an issue in their home. But the biggest problem developed in my private life.

In my teen years I was very shy. I never had much of a relationship with girls because I was afraid of their rejection of me. My image of myself was so poor that I "knew" everyone else felt the same way about me. I assumed that to ask a girl out would make me too vulnerable. My fears ranged from a simple "No" to the fear of someone's laughing at me when I asked her to go out.

But the problem with that shyness was that I didn't lessen my curiosity of the female anatomy. Instead it forced me "underground" to a world of secretivity and exploration, into the world of pornography and self-stimulation.

In his private world Pastor Paul found "no ridicule, no risk," he said. But he soon was hooked on pornographic magazines as he tried to escape his fears and supply his sexual drive. He became uncertain, and his habits affected his ministry. Once, as a youth pastor, he tried to counsel a man at the end of the church service. Paul took him aside and asked about his need, and "he handed me a note that simply stated, 'Masturbation.' That shocked me! I had no idea how to help him. I quickly prayed for him and dismissed him. I regret my actions now, but no one ever told me what to say to people who need prayer about sexual issues.

"In hindsight, no wonder that I was so shocked. I was still dealing with the problem and the guilt myself. It took me years to get this under control. . . . The issue of escapism and how to handle stress was what I had to learn, and with God's help I am still learning it."

How many Pauls are there today? How many Christians sit in their pews week after week, sing hymns and praise choruses, listen to sermons and take notes, and inside feel dirty and hypocritical because of present or past inability to deal with their sexual drives? How many are longing to hear a positive way to deal with their sexuality but are too ashamed to ask for help?

COMMON ATTEMPTS TO HELP

Christian singles have come a long way since Paul's college days. Young men and women can sit together in Christian college cafeterias, sex and AIDS awareness seminars are common, and once taboo topics can now be discussed in churches. Unfortunately, though, the answers that are given to our young people and adult singles are, in my opinion, still inadequate. They do not present any positive motivation to remain celibate. Positive guidelines for single sexuality, especially ways to deal with sexual temptation, are essential yet lacking.

Two of these common (yet insufficient) approaches to teaching abstinence to teens and adults are what I call *the ostrich option* and *the detour dilemma*. As you read about these two negative approaches, think back to the things you were taught about singles and sexuality. Is one of these approaches similar to what you have been taught? Is it the way you have been trying to keep your sexual impulses under control?

The Ostrich Option

Teens and single adults are still being told to handle their sexual urges by avoiding them. This really isn't so different from what Pastor Paul was taught in the '50s. The main difference is that, in Paul's day, even the discussion of sexuality was considered sinful. Today, it's not considered a sin to talk about sex and to admit that we have sex drives, but the answer is still, "Don't think about it, don't go to places or watch things that will make you feel it, and above all don't do it."

This was painfully obvious to me as I listened to a tape of a popular youth minister lecturing about sex at a high school convention. His main message was, "Don't get yourself into situations where you will be sexually tempted." He gave a personal example:

"When I travel to speak at conferences, I am always careful when I go into my hotel room for the first time," the speaker said. "The first thing I do is take the movie listing off the TV and turn it face down so that I can't read the movies. Then I call the front desk and ask them to block all movie rentals from my room. That way I can't watch any movies that might excite me sexually. You gotta plan ahead and avoid anything that will cause you to fall."

Now I agree that many movies are harmful to watch, but I was saddened that this leader's main message to his teens about sex was "avoid it!" In our culture, that simply isn't possible. What are teens to do when they are watching a football game and the cameraman focuses in on the cheerleaders or some cute coeds in bikini tops? What should they do when, as they watch the evening news, a report about a series of sex crimes is covered in lurid detail or a clip is aired from a Chippendales Nightclub for women? How should they react when they are walking down a street and suddenly a woman dressed very provocatively rounds the corner and walks right towards them? Are they to prevent all such temptations from happening?

No, of course not. That would be impossible. By the time they see such a woman or man or hear a lurid report, even if they turn their eyes away or turn off the TV, the image is already fixed in their minds. And the more they try to forget it, the easier it is to become obsessed about it.

In all honesty, I did not consider his suggestion to the teens to be in their best interest. Rather than learning to control their impulses, they were being taught to protect themselves from all temptation. Try as they may, no one can insulate himself or herself from sexual temptation. As with the ostrich who puts his head in the sand to avoid trouble, the trouble is still there, even though he can't see it.

Some singles avoid dealing with their own sexuality by making themselves unattractive to others. Some do this by overeating or by excessive under-eating. Others dress poorly or practice poor hygiene. Still others maintain a negative, unattractive demeanor and attitude. The methods chosen and combinations used are as numerous as are the men and women who are fearful of their sexuality. They try to avoid the issue by somehow hiding it or making it seem unappealing. But in the end, this approach does not solve the root problem. Like a bandage over a cancerous growth, it may hide the problem, but sooner or later the cancer will destroy everything. Avoidance simply is not the answer.

Jodie began dating at fifteen. At seventeen she had a couple of bad dating experiences and wanted to end her dating, so she began to eat. "[I was] convinced that dating was not for me, and I subconsciously gave it up. I still acted like I wanted to date, but I immediately gained thirty pounds [an effective method of keeping most men at arm's length] and began believing all men were evil. This, of course, worked very well to keep me from dating. I realize now with hindsight that this was a protective measure for someone who at the time was not very psychologically sophisticated but did not want to be hurt anymore."

The Detour Dilemma

Another popular suggestion is for singles to harness their sexual energy and use it in some other way or area. One singles pastor told his singles that the solution to sexual frustration was to exercise more. He said, "When I feel tempted, I go out and run a couple of miles. If I'm really tempted, I run five or six. I find that if I run long enough I can use up the sexual energy in a positive way." Yes, you guessed it. This particular singles pastor now runs marathons. But not everyone can run marathons, or swim laps, or lift weights as a way of diverting sexual energy.

Sometimes the detour approach takes on overtly Christian content, such as the divorced evangelist who dealt with his sexuality by "spending more time reading the Word." To be sure, the Bible is an excellent source of strength and comfort, and reading it will deeply nurture us as believers. But what this evangelist didn't realize was that he was merely replacing his former addictions on cocaine and sex with a new addiction. He was able, for a while, to throw his energies into Bible study, but after a time this became humdrum. Interestingly, he finally gave up on Christianity and the Bible, saying that it just wasn't powerful enough to deal with the real world.

One charming retreat speaker gave her audience a different route for this detour approach. She said, "Whenever a Christian lady asks me how as a single I deal with sex, I just tell her, 'Honey, get busy for the Lord. If you serve Him day and night like I do, you won't have the time or energy to worry about sex.'" Again, this sounds spiritual and sacrificial, but it too is insufficient. Rather than producing balanced, whole Christians who are able to control their thoughts and impulses, it produces worn-out, burned-out, tired Christians. And they are probably worse off than before, because in their weakened condition they are more susceptible to temptation.

Exercise, obsessive Bible study, and even "getting busy for the Lord" are just examples of sublimation. Sublimation is a defense mechanism that channels forbidden impulses into more socially accepted outlets. An easy way to visualize sublimation is to imagine that a deep pothole has formed on a busy highway. Construction crews put up barricades to keep drivers from driving on that road, and they erect detour signs to guide the drivers along alternate routes. The detour allows drivers to continue to function safely. In the same way, the unconscious often places barriers in front of unacceptable desires and redirects that energy toward more acceptable outlets.

As a temporary approach, sublimation may be helpful, but as a long-term solution it fails again and again. Let's return to the road crew illustration: If a pothole appears in the road, it certainly is wise to temporarily direct drivers away from the danger and onto an alternate route. But sooner or later, the pothole should be repaired so the normal traffic flow can resume.

What would happen if, rather than fixing potholes, our local maintenance teams decided to make every detour permanent? Chaos would result. Soon the detour would itself develop potholes; a detour for the detour would have to be erected, and so on. Our communities would end up tangled messes of redirected routes. It would be virtually impossible to get anywhere efficiently. A standstill would result, because all the roads would have potholes and none would be repaired.

I remember experiencing this type of traffic nightmare in the summer of 1977, as a young college student traveling through the Soviet satellite countries behind the Iron Curtain. I was a part of a team of college students who were trying to bring Bibles into the Eastern bloc countries. We made it through each crossing without trouble but then met with a difficulty that we hadn't expected. The roads and highway infrastructure of these countries was an absolute mess—crumbling roads and potholes everywhere. There were detours upon detours, as the repairs never seemed to find completion.

As the navigator for the group, I often despaired of ever finding our destinations because the detours would not lead us to the right roads. The much better option for the local authorities would have been to fix the potholes quickly so the most efficient routes could be open to traffic. Similarly, the better option in our personal lives is to deal directly with our sexuality. If we respond to temptation or sexual frustration by creating permanent detours around those areas, new problems will soon appear on the detour.

For instance, we may get busy for the Lord and choose to serve God in a ministry area of our local church. But what will we do when we meet an attractive member of the opposite sex in that new ministry group? The inability to deal with sexual frustration is still there, and we have not learned how to handle it positively. So we have to create a new detour within the current detour. We may say to ourselves, "OK, I'll be a part of this ministry, but I'll try not to sit close to that person." Later, it's not just physical proximity that's a problem, but also visual proximity. So we decide to not even look in that person's direction, and the sublimation chaos deepens. What a mess! Our lives become a jumble of detours.

This is the dilemma we place ourselves in when sublimation is used as a permanent solution rather than a temporary option. For single Christians, the sexual issue cannot be avoided forever; the potholes need to be positively dealt with and permanently fixed.

In spite of the popularity of the ostrich and detour approaches to single sexuality, neither avoidance nor sublimation deals with the real issue. Instead, they just delay and mask the fact that singles are sexual people. Singles need more—they need a positive reason to remain celibate and a positive way to handle temptation when it comes.

God has left our sex switches on for a reason. In His wisdom He has chosen not to switch singles off for a while sexually. He has a reason for doing this, and it is not mere biology.

MORE THAN JUST BIOLOGY

Many singles claim, "Well, God created me with these parts, so I'm going to use them. He created me to be a physical person, and sex is just as natural as breathing or eating. It wouldn't be wise for me to stop breathing, would it? And eating is a physical drive too. If I stop eating, I will destroy this body. Sex isn't something I can just turn off, it's a natural part of life. In spite of what the Bible says, I feel the body is good and sex is good. After all, whatever is natural is good."

They are saying sex is a biological function and unavoidable. This is the naturalistic, evolutionary view of sexuality. Since we are mere animals, this argument says, we should not deprive ourselves of bodily pleasures. Even more important, we must not deprive ourselves of sexual pleasure because it is our duty to procreate and keep our genetic inheritance alive.

But surely there is a deeper reason for our sexuality than mere biology; there must be a more profound explanation to our desire for intimacy than just the evolutionary survival of the species. Sex must be more than just a bestial attraction and a response. Of course, in a culture in which God at best is seen as irrelevant, and at worst is seen as dead, the human being is reduced to a merely animal level. Accept the idea that God does not exist, and you need not worry about such things as the spiritual or transcendent. All of life is reduced to purely physical, animal terms.

Shakespeare, in the tragedy *Othello*, had one of his characters adopt the same low view of sexuality. Iago, Othello's trusted officer who betrays that trust, scoffed at anyone who thought that sex was a transcendent experience and denied that it was in any way elevated above a purely physical level. For Iago, sex was all "goats and monkeys." In other words, it was a purely animal act and made clear the fundamental bestial level that humanity, for him, could not rise above.

This reduction of our humanness to a purely physical level is reflected in the modern industry of pornography, which treats sexuality and bodies as mere objects to photograph and display as one would any other physical object. The word *pornography* comes from the Greek word *porneia*, whose root, *porn*, means 'to sell,' and was first applied to prostitutes who used their bodies for financial profit. *Pornography*, true to its etymological heritage, means sex for sale.

Sadly, today the pornographic industry is not the only industry that uses sex for a profit. Sex is used to sell movies; many producers believe a G-rated movie will probably not make the profit that it would if some steamy sex scenes were added and the rating changed to an R. Not only does TV and radio advertising use sex to sell products, but the very content of the most popular shows is unabashedly sexual. Everything from hair care products to food, from clothing to cars, from vitamins to vacations uses sex to sell its wares. It almost seems as if our whole culture uses sex for a profit.

A REFLECTION OF GOD

The Bible proclaims loudly that we are not mere animals, naked and bestial. Neither are we sexual simply on a physical, animalistic level. Theologically, there is a hidden purpose behind our creation as sexual persons. Understanding this hidden purpose helps us to do two things: value ourselves more and learn a positive way to handle sexual temptation. The good news is that our sexuality is not merely biological or bestial but instead is a reflection of God.

This truth is not buried in some obscure passage in the Old Testament or in one of those small, prophetic books that few can find or pronounce. The reason for our sexuality is not embarrassing and therefore relegated to a footnote somewhere. Instead, it is given clearly in the very first chapter in the first book of the Bible, right there on page one—Genesis 1:27. Many scholars see this verse as the culmination, the climax of the passage.

The Hebrew writer of the book of Genesis, in the first chapter, was saying that in the beginning God created everything. After He created most things, He climaxed his creative actions with His best work ever—man and woman. The greatest of His creations and the goal of the whole creation effort is given in verse 27:

> So God created man in his own image,
> in the image of God he created him,
> male and female he created them.

A LITTLE LESSON IN HEBREW POETRY

Before analyzing the Genesis 1:27 passage, we must first note a few things about Hebrew poetry. Though this may seem at first glance to have nothing to do with sexuality, it will become helpful for us in a moment (so hang in there for a few paragraphs and some fun diagrams). Hebrew poetry is quite different from the poetic sounds and patterns we are used to. Instead of emphasizing rhyme and meter, as does much English poetry, it often uses *parallel structure*; that is, each line is parallel to another line in a certain way. Parallelism is a beautiful and complex type of poetry, and fortunately for us one that survives translation well.

One type of parallelism is *synthetic parallelism*. Here, the first line is directly parallel to the next line, but its themes would be further supported and explained by the following line. An example of this is Psalm 1:1:

> Blessed is the man
> who does not walk in the counsel of the wicked,
> or stand in the way of sinners,
> or sit in the seat of scoffers.

Contrary to some energetic expositors, the last three lines do not describe the three different types of men that a godly person ought to avoid. Instead, the three lines add together in a synthetic way to give a stronger and more powerful expression of the central point: Don't hang around with bad guys. By repeating themes in exact order, the writers could bring emphasis to the important thoughts, which was important before the days of underlining and bold type.

It's sort of like the father who really wants to make a point to his son who has just wrecked the family car and wants to borrow the other car. Dad says in exasperation, "I don't want you to drive the car, I don't want you to sit in the car, I don't even want you to look at the car!" As we all quickly realize, the father is not outlining in precise, scientific detail three things that he wants the son to avoid. Instead, through synthetic parallelism he is driving his point home: "I'm upset, and you're going to have to walk for a while."

Another type of Hebrew parallelism is *antithetical parallelism*. In this type the main point was made by saying the theme first positively and then negatively (An example of this is Proverbs 3:5, "Trust in the Lord with all your heart, and do not lean on your own understanding.")

A third type of parallelism is called *chiasm* (pronounced ki-asm), which means a sort of crossing. Here the same themes are switched in adjacent lines, the switch drawing attention to the themes and sometimes bringing one into prominent position. If the switching themes were connected by lines, an X would form between the lines. The word *chiasm* actually is derived from the Greek letter X, called *chi*. An example of chiasm is found in the two opening lines of Amos 5:14–15.

> Seek good, not evil...
>
> Hate evil, love good...

The same theme is expressed by both lines, but the order of the two parts is reversed. The crossing of themes lends power to the poetry.

THE POETIC STRUCTURE OF GENESIS 1:27

Genesis 1:27 uses both synthetic parallelism and chiasm; let's take an in-depth look at the verse. First, we will underline the subjects, verbs, and direct objects in each line and connect them:

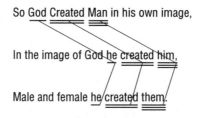

This part was really easy. The Hebrew writer did not want us to miss his parallelism, so he used the same verb (created), the same subject (God/he), and a simple object (man/him/them). This is a normal example of synthetic parallelism, in which each theme corresponds to its match in the next line. We can clearly see the flow of the poetic lines. It is against this flow that the poet will bring to the fore his main point.

We also have an easy time with the chiasm (crossing of ideas) between the first and second lines. There, the phrases "in his own image" and "in the image of God" cross with the phrase "God created man" and "he created him."

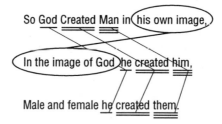

It is as if the chiasm has thrust the phrase "in the image of God" onto center stage. It has been brought forward to claim our attention. This is exactly what was intended, for the author's big surprise is waiting for us in the synthetic parallelism that remains between lines two and three. There we are told what the image of God actually is:

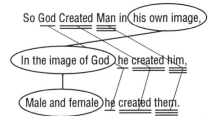

So God Created Man in his own image,

In the image of God he created him,

Male and female he created them.

The point of this poetic structure is to strongly emphasize that the image of God is reflected in our creation as male and female. The message is clear: the image of God is reflected in the male-female relationship. What exactly does it mean to reflect the image of God in the male-female relationship, and how can that help us to deal with sexual temptations?

THE IMAGE OF GOD

Past generations have speculated about the image of God, the *imago Dei*, assuming that the image was our souls, our original righteousness, and especially our minds. This last and most popular notion about minds simply meant that we are in God's image because we are the only rational, abstractly thinking animals. However, we now know that animals are capable of some rational, abstract thinking too. Koko the gorilla, for instance, has a vocabulary of more than five hundred words and can create her own words by putting two words together to form compound nouns. If humans are distinct from other animals, it cannot be due to our rational capacity alone.

Dietrich Bonhoeffer and Karl Barth, two twentieth-century theologians, saw a different message in the poetic structure of Genesis 1:27: the image of God was expressed in our creation as male and female. Bonhoeffer said this expressed an analogy of relationship (*analogia relationis*). In other words, the analogy, or likeness, between God and humans is relationship, the ability to relate. And Barth described sexuality as the "God-like" in us. By this he did not mean that God was sexually differentiated. Instead, our sexuality displays our ability and inclination to be relational people. We are created with the inborn ability and need to relate to others.

It is no wonder that we desire so deeply, then, to find intimacy. It is God's created intention for each of us. We are designed to be in relationship; we are driven to develop intimate friendships. The image of God in us, according to Genesis 1:27, is our ability to relate and share intimacy. It is, therefore, when we love others and allow ourselves to be loved that we most reflect the image of God.

THE GOD OF LOVE

But why is the image of God reflected most when we are relating to others intimately? The answer to this question is subtle in its simplicity, yet also beautiful in its profundity. God's image is reflected when we love naturally, because above all else, God's nature is to love. "God is love," as 1 John 4:8 proclaims.

Here we are touching on a very deep truth, one that theologians for two millennia have described by the word *Trinity*. The idea of the Trinity is confusing to most of us, for our logical minds cannot compute the meaning of three-in-one. For some this has been a stumbling block to faith. Attempts to explain the Trinity by analogies of ice and eggs are incomplete and not fully satisfying.

Instead, there is a deeper significance to the Trinity, to the notion of a God who is three-in-one. Within the very being of God is the reality of a shared intimacy and love. There is a communion within the being of God. God does not just love others; He shares love within Himself. Among the Father, the Son, and the Spirit are fellowship and friendship. In His very being love is expressed. Thus 1 John 4:8 says "God is love," and not merely "God loves." This is why the notion of Trinity is so vital. A monotheistic, nontrinitarian God loves others, but is not loving within Himself. A triune God, though, displays a reciprocal love and intimacy among the members of the Trinity.

We humans are created to share such reciprocal love. We each are designed by God to be involved in loving, mutual, intimate relationships. In other words, when we enter into deep and loving friendships, we do so because we were created to be relational. We weren't meant to live as hermits or in solitary confinement. God created us in His own relational image so that we would—in spite of the hazards and pain—develop intimate relationships with Himself and others.

And in a wonderful way, this drive towards relationships is a positive tool God uses to prod us to quality friendships. Our sexuality is actually a gift from God that can help us develop true friendships, as we shall see in the next chapter.

Questions for Discussion
1. How many Christians do you think sit in their pews, sing hymns and praise choruses, listen to sermons and take notes, but inside feel dirty and hypocritical because of present or past inability to deal with their sexual drives? (Circle your answer.)

   10%   25%   50%   75%   100%

   Why do they feel that way?

2. Why do you think Christians have such a hard time being honest with one another about sexual struggles?

3. How do singles you know live out the ostrich option? That is, what lengths do they go to to avoid any situations that might be sexually tempting?

4. How do singles you know live out the detour dilemma? What do they do to channel their sexual drives and energies into other areas? For instance, do they exercise, cook, shop, serve other people?

5. Do these singles' detours work as temporary defense mechanisms? Why or why not? Do they work as permanent defense mechanisms? Why or why not?

6. You have been created in the image of God. In the past, what did you always assume that "the image of God" meant? How does it make you feel to know that God created you to be a relational person? How will this affect your friendships? How will it affect the way you spend your time?

CHAPTER SEVEN

WHAT IS THE HIDDEN PURPOSE BEHIND SINGLE SEXUALITY?

We have learned that God created us to be relational people. He wants us to develop strong, loving, intimate friendships with Himself and with others. But there is a problem with this, a problem that singles especially have discovered through the pain of divorce, bereavement, and disappointment. The problematic discovery is this: mutual love and intimacy are not easy things for humans to achieve. The road to love is long and hard. Though the destination is wonderful, the way is perilous. Many of us have crashed on this road and have been deeply hurt and scarred in the process.

HESITANT AND HARDENED HEARTS

Many are afraid to make new attempts at love, knowing full well that they might crash and burn once more. Once deeply hurt or betrayed, it is very difficult to summon the courage to try again at love, to trust others, or to even trust ourselves. After an particularly painful experience, some singles conclude that the risks of love are just too great. They are tempted to think it may be safer to stay off the road and out of love. Their motto is "If I don't love again, at least I can't get hurt."

A bitter experience can also lead to disillusionment and hardened hearts. Though once soft and open to love, their hearts have become stone cold and hard, impervious to pain or penetration. And this is not an accident. A hard heart is not something that happens in us without our awareness and approval. We don't wake up one morning and with surprise discover that we have a hardened heart. No, a hardened heart is an act of the will. We choose to harden our hearts. That's why the Bible repeatedly warns, "Do not harden your hearts" (Psalm 95:8; Mark 10:5; Hebrews 3:8, 15; 4:7; etc.). It's a condition that can be avoided.

These attitudes—hesitant and hardened hearts—are very common among singles. We all have heard (and maybe have said) such statements as "I'll never trust a man again" or "I've had enough of women—never again!" I remember one Southern California talk-show host saying on the air (after his second divorce), "A person has got to be crazy to get married. I've told my friends, and now I'm telling you listeners: if you ever hear me say that I'm getting married again, I want you to get your gun and blow my head off!" I gathered from this that he was "hesitant" about new relationships.

God has created us in such a way as to prevent this kind of hesitancy and withdrawal from love. He does not want us to give up on the search for intimacy. He desires that we form positive and nurturing relationships with Himself and others. But to do this is scary. As with a person who is afraid to get back on a horse after being thrown, after a negative relationship it is very tough to get back in the saddle of romance. Rather than a safe, easy ride, love looks more like a bucking bronco! So if God wants us to love again, He has His work cut out for Him. He has to combat this powerful tendency to withdraw from the rigors of love.

SEXUALITY AS A SPIRITUAL GIFT

In order to fight this, God created us with a built-in guarantee that we would not give up on love. Our sexuality is this guarantee. Sexuality is God's insurance that we will continue to be relational individuals. Rather than withdrawing from others, sexuality continues to draw us to others. Rather than refusing to work on relationships, our sex drives insure that we will do the work necessary to establish relationships. Created in God's image, with a need for personal relationships, we have received our sexual drives as one means of compelling us into relationships. Thus our sexuality is a gift from God, one of his ways that we will seek loving relationships with those different from us.

Like ships that have weathered terrible storms on the open sea, some singles have been damaged—even sunk at times. They come into the harbor of singleness badly in need of repair and terribly afraid of ever venturing out to sea again. As the saying goes, "A ship in a harbor is safe, but that is not what ships were built for." They were built to sail the open seas. In the same way, people removed from relationships are "safe," but that is not what we were created for. We were created to love and be loved, to reflect the very image of God.

Author and psychologist Scott Peck argues that our sex drives are placed deep within our genetic makeup to ensure we will marry and reproduce. In his best-selling book *The Road Less Traveled,* Peck writes,

> The sexual specificity of the phenomenon [of falling in love] leads me to suspect that it is a genetically determined instinctual component of mating behavior. . . . Or, to put it in another, rather crass way, falling in love is a trick that our genes pull on our otherwise perceptive mind to hoodwink or trap us into marriage. . . . Without this trick . . . many of us who are happily or unhappily married today would have retreated in wholehearted terror from the realism of the marriage vows.[1]

Peck takes a common secular view: the sex drive is the evolutionary, biological guarantee that our species will continue to propagate itself. This also is the thesis behind the popular book *Mystery Dance,* written by Lynn Margulis and Dorion Sagan. Believing that sexuality is the mere result of evolution, they investigate every detail of human sexuality to discover how it added to the chances of genetic survival. Starting from their major premise—that natural selection is the motivating force behind every evolutionary development—they go to great lengths to attach to each sexual part a rationale.

Such an approach is both arbitrary and incredibly diminishing. Human sexuality is reduced to survival techniques. But even worse, the drive towards relationship and intimacy is relegated to the animal level. Though their approach may satisfy scientific analysis, it fails the course in theological anthropology. Humanness is more than just mere creatureliness. Even our physical bodies are not just the result of genetic advantage; they too reflect a design and a Designer.

Just as sexuality is more than an animal instinct, so too our sex drive is not merely biological but reflects a theological purpose. God knew we would shy away from the demands of achieving intimacy, so He created us in such a way that we would be forced to work towards intimacy in spite of our fears. Our sexuality motivates us to be relational people. Margulis and Sagan are heading in the wrong direction; all of life cannot be explained by the evolutionary hypothesis because it lacks any appreciation for transcendence. Peck, though appreciative of the transcendence, misses the deeper significance of the sexual drive. The sexual impulse does keep us involved in relationships, but it is not, as he supposes, a trick that a fully functioning, rational person would recognize and avoid. The marriage commitment and the desire for monogamy are not irrational. Instead, they reflect the deep drive implanted within us by God to insure that we don't miss out on the very best part of life—the intimacy of healthy relationships. It is God's way to motivate us to develop loving, committed relationships in spite of the difficulties and pain involved. That does not mean that God necessarily wants you to be married; it means he wants you to accept the risk in developing relationships with the opposite sex (just as there are risks and losses in developing friendships with the same sex).

Sexual attraction then can be seen as a sort of spiritual gift, even though sexuality doesn't appear in the spiritual gift lists in the New Testament and won't show up on one of the various spiritual gifts tests. But I maintain, nonetheless, that it is one of God's greatest gifts to human beings, married or single.

THE DRIVE TOWARD INTIMACY

Humans are physically drawn to others not just to satisfy physical desire and not merely to keep the species alive. In the drama of human history, sexual desire and procreation are really just minor players— publicity seeking primadonnas who, much to their disappointment, are only given bit parts. The major character, the real star on the stage of human history, corresponds to the major theme: the desire for interpersonal intimacy. The most important actor is the hunger for interpersonal closeness that most strongly attracts us to one another. It is the thirst for a communion of souls that motivates us to love in spite of the fear of failure.

God, as we learned in the last chapter, did not create us as mere animals but chose to reflect in us His own ability to relate, love, and experience intimacy. This is real drama; here we find true passion and purpose. All of human history is the unfolding episode of how humans have loved and related to one another. From the very first, humans have lived their lives with one another, founding families, tribes, communities, and countries.

The Bible calls this *koinonia*, which is usually translated *fellowship*, but the word can also be translated as *partnership, participation,* or *communion*. The root, *koinos*, means "common, belonging to several," so the basic meaning of fellowship is to have something in common, to share a common bond. The early church gathered together, for this very reason. "They devoted themselves to the apostles' teaching and to the fellowship, to the breaking of bread and to prayer" (Acts 2:42).

Fellowship, we must note in this day of church shopping and hopping, was not an optional extra for those early Christians. They *devoted* themselves to fellowship. It was the very goal of the Christian community. "We proclaim to you what we have seen and heard, so that you also may have fellowship with us. And our fellowship is with the Father and with His Son, Jesus Christ. We write this to make our joy complete" (1 John 1:3–4). Again we see that fellowship is something that we not only have together but with a relational God, and a life of fellowship is the only way to find complete joy.

Sexual desire is part of that drive toward intimacy. Modern science has made major strides toward ensuring fertility outside of actual sexual relations, yet that has not diminished sexual desire. With today's techniques of artificial insemination, test tube babies, and sperm banks, if our main desire was merely to have offspring to ensure our genetic survival, the need for sexual relations between people would presumably lessen. Obviously, that has not happened. Though we can have kids without sexual contact, humans aren't exercising that option except when forced to by infertility.

This is also why the world of sex industries, such as pornography, self-stimulation toys, and nude bars, will never replace the desire for a loving partner. The sexual drive is not fulfilled by mere orgasm or titillation; it is only fulfilled by interpersonal intimacy. This is because sex isn't just physical release—it is also interpersonal connection. We are not driven just to have orgasms; we are driven to experience intimacy.

As Smedes says in *Sex for Christians*, "Beyond the glandular impulse, the human sexual urge is always toward another person. . . . As bodies we experience the urge first in the vague sense of physical restlessness; as persons we experience it in the desire for a person."[2] Neither pornography, sex shows, nor 900 number sex hotlines are ultimately fulfilling, because they reduce people to mere sex objects, to the base animal level.

The sex drive is not just orgasm- or excitement-oriented. It is, as Smedes says, person-oriented. The deepest reason we are drawn into relationships is not to experience orgasms. It is to express our original design to develop interpersonal relationships of love. As a result, the drive toward intimacy is ultimately other-person centered. The crucial factor in reflecting the image of God is not sexual involvement—it is relational involvement.

Thus singles, sometimes to their own surprise, are motivated to love even after painful experiences. Of course, it may take several months or even years before we are ready to venture out in building a loving relationship again. It takes time to ready oneself to love again. It takes healing before one can risk vulnerability.

But sooner or later, most singles give love another shot. The battered woman who exclaimed, "I'll never trust another man again!" probably will change her mind and choose to try at love again. The man who loudly said, "I've had enough of women—never again," may reconsider. Chances are that he too will decide that he would like some involvement with women after all. Even the radio talk-show host who refused to give marriage one more shot decided to get married again. And then he begged, on the air, for his friends and listeners to release him from his hasty request that they shoot him.

INTIMACY AND WHOLENESS
AS A SINGLE PERSON

With all of this talk of relationships, it might seem as if one must be married to experience this type of intimacy. It is easy to blithely assume that such relational closeness can only happen in a marriage. If that is so, then one must be married to fully reflect the image of God. Is this the case? Do singles have to get married to experience this deep interpersonal intimacy that I have been talking about?

In any discussion of this topic, a never-married person will always ask this kind of question: "I want to experience intimacy, and I feel that in order to experience it I've got to get married. Right?" Those in the room who were previously married usually respond to this question with a knowing grin or a gentle laugh. Then one of them will kindly say, "I've got news for you. Marriage does not guarantee intimacy." How true. Just as sex does not guarantee intimacy, neither does marriage guarantee a communion of souls. Of course, deep intimacy can be found in some marriages, but it is a naive mistake to assume all marriages are intimate.

It is also a mistake to assume that singles cannot reflect the image of God in unmarried friendships. Two people need not be physical to be vulnerable. They need not experience intercourse to experience interpersonal closeness. Singles who relate to others in mutual love can fully reflect the image of God.

Actually, the most important aspects of intimacy have little to do with physical touching. Commitment, trust, loyalty, honesty, burden-sharing, forgiveness—these are the nutrients that feed intimacy. Because of this, intimacy can occur without disrobing. In the absence of sexual touching, intimacy can blossom. It can be a very hardy plant, given the right conditions. As Smedes put it:

> Can a male be a whole person without a personal relationship with a woman? We must remember that male and female can and do relate to each other without touching each other's skin, just as they can be skin-close without relating as persons. . . . Virgins . . . can experience personal wholeness by giving themselves to other persons without physical sex. Through a life of self-giving—which is at the heart of sexual union—they become whole persons. They capture the essence without the usual form. [3]

This notion of personal wholeness is a crucial part of the single adult pilgrimage. Too often we singles feel we are incomplete without marriage, that in the absence of some significant other we are not whole. Something is missing. So some of us attach ourselves to another incomplete person, hoping that together our two halves will add up to a whole. This coincides with that common phrase spoken by married people where a spouse is called a half-person as in, "Here comes my better half." Is this true? Are singles half-people, who need to find their other half in order to experience wholeness?

It is easy to give in to this feeling of incompleteness and decide that, "Well, I'm just a half-person and need someone else to complete me. I had better find someone else, or I will never feel whole." But, as one single pointed out, relationships are more like multiplication than addition. In multiplication, two halves don't make a whole: $\frac{1}{2} \times \frac{1}{2} = \frac{1}{4}$. In this math, if two half-people get together, they end up with one-quarter of God's potential for their lives.

It's not even enough to find a whole person to marry if first we don't develop our own wholeness, because $\frac{1}{2} \times 1 = \frac{1}{2}$. If a half-person marries a whole person, they still end up with just one-half of the potential that God intended them to have. The only way to insure that we will find relational wholeness is to take the time as singles to develop our own sense of personal wholeness in Christ. Then two whole people can together experience the full measure of God's potential for their friendship or relationship, because $1 \times 1 = 1$.

After all this talk of being relational people and needing intimacy to reflect God's image, it is easy to mistakenly assume that wholeness will only develop in marriage. That's why it is crucial to understand that singles can develop into whole people without marriage and without sexual contact. In the Bible we find several strong examples of singles who were whole people. Jesus Himself is the supreme example—His singleness did not prevent Him from developing intimate relationships with His heavenly Father and with others. He was, to be sure, the whole person *par excellence*. Another example is the apostle Paul, who emphasized his singleness in his first letter to the Corinthians. From their examples and from many other singles mentioned in the Bible, we can conclude that wholeness is possible for unmarried persons. Wholeness is a reachable goal for singles. To sum up, wholeness does not require sexual involvement with someone else, but it does require relational involvement.

Then how does the issue of sexuality and our sex drives fit into the issue of single wholeness? Is the sex drive our blessing or curse as singles? Does it help or hinder us on the path to personal wholeness in Christ? I am claiming that the sex drive, contrary to first impressions, can become an aid in this development of wholeness. As we have learned in this chapter, the sex drive helps singles to keep in the relationship arena. Even after singles have been burned, they are motivated to give love a try again. In this manner, sexuality is just a helper in the process of becoming whole people. If it helps in an appropriate, controlled way, relational intimacy is enhanced. But if it asserts itself and becomes a dominant theme, it can destroy the relational intimacy it was created to assist.

It's easy to confuse intimacy with sexual relations and to settle for a sexual liaison instead of a friendship. In "A Single Speaks," a woman describes how she left the imitation intimacy and sought the real thing. She found it by starting to look for her next friends instead of for a lover. That's the path to true intimacy between people: seek friendships. When you seek friendships instead of a mate, you may end up with both.

A SINGLE SPEAKS

I have listened to the tapes on "The Positive Side of Single Sexuality," and after a few sleepless nights and a lot of praying, I have broken up with my boyfriend, or I should say we have reorganized our relationship.

Every time we were together, I would leave feeling low, lower than any bargain basement table could get. He has always treated me right. Sex never came into his mind until I put it there. It didn't hit me until one night driving home from his house . . . I was treating him like a bargain basement table. I was trying to get him to come down to my level. I was not in love with him, and he says he loves me . . . . I thought maybe if we got physical, love would come. Wrong!!

When I first heard you speak at a retreat several years ago, you spoke on intimacy, and you said to look for your next friend, not your mate/lover. . . , [that] a friend is for life and if God blesses you with one . . . you will have a special gift from God. I have told this to a lot of my friends, and I have it in my singles newsletter.

God has blessed me with many friends, and at times I want more than just a good friend. I know that I have to keep everything on track and with God's help I will.

TWISTED SEXUALITY

The fact that God has chosen not to switch off the sex drive in single adults, then, is not an error in judgment on His part. For singles, the sex drive is not a curse, nor is it something to avoid or repress. It is not without benefit. There is a hidden opportunity for singles as they are sexually attracted to others.

An opportunity? A good thing that I still find myself physically attracted to others? You may regard such attractions and urges as disabilities and hindrances. Sometimes we even consider our physical attraction to others as an evil impulse conjured up by the evil forces. Any sexual urges before marriage are seen as naughty and dirty. This is not just a modern viewpoint, by the way. Throughout the history of Christianity, many spiritually devoted Christians believed that their sexual impulses were totally impure and in need of mortification.

For instance, the church Father Origen taught that the body (especially sexuality) was the seat of all sadness and frustration. It limited humans from achieving true Christlikeness. The Christian life, then, was a battle against the body. Origen practiced what he preached and had himself castrated when he was about twenty, but his reason for doing this is commonly misunderstood. He did not do it to make himself immune to temptation. As Brown points out, "Postpubertal castration merely made a man infertile; it was, in itself, no guarantee of chastity."[4] What Origen really wanted was even more drastic—to stop being a man. Without a beard, he would belong to neither sex and thus could be a living example of release from the sexual determinism.[5]

This attitude is very much alive today among Christians, and it creates enormous problems for dating couples and newlyweds. They have been taught to view sexual impulses as evil before marriage and suddenly good after marriage. Those who believe this think that evil is the source of sexual urges for years and years, and that then all of a sudden God takes over.

Yet after a lifetime of identifying certain urges as evil, it is almost impossible to switch overnight and view these same urges as holy.

Many newlyweds find this confusion to be enormously difficult, often limiting sexual fulfillment in marriage. As one newly married man said, "I like it so far, but I can't stop feeling guilty about it. I mean, sex has been a bad thing my whole life. And now, all of the sudden, I'm supposed to believe it's clean. I'm confused." His problem is a common one—if sex was inappropriate yesterday, how can we convince ourselves that it is appropriate today?

This problem is not sexual; it is theological. Sexual impulses before marriage are not evil—they are merely physical impulses, chemical reactions, within our amazing, God-designed bodies. But these physical feelings can be turned and twisted into an evil use. As the apostle James says, they can become lust when we allow them to carry us away and entice us (James 1:13–15). Sexual attractiveness was created by God but (like many of His good and perfect gifts) can be misused for poor purposes.

TOO CLOSE, TOO SOON

Thinking that sex can promote intimacy, some singles hop in the sack too quickly. This misuse of sexuality twists the whole relationship-building process designed by God and often makes the process infinitely more difficult. Couples with great potential can sabotage their future by sexual involvement too early. As one woman said, "Gene and I could have been great together. But we destroyed our future by getting involved too soon sexually. Before I knew it I was pregnant, and the pressures upon us were just too great for our young relationship to endure. The baby was born, but our love died. I can see now that we killed it."

How often I have seen this happen (the tendency to get too close, too soon) to Christian couples. I have no doubt that in many cases it was God who led the two people together, and they began to experience a relational intimacy reflective of the very image of God. But before they had a chance to develop a solid foundation for their relationship, they jumped into bed together. The weight of sexual intimacy was just too much for the new relationship, and their romantic dream became a quagmire of difficulty, conflict, and disappointment. Sex too soon puts too much stress on a new relationship.

Let's think about this in terms of the analogy of a young couple building their dream house. Here in southern California, all the homes have concrete slab foundations. Even if the couple have a great piece of land, a wonderful design, and all the materials and labor needed, they still have to wait for the foundation to dry before going any further.

What if they became so excited about the house, so anxious to enjoy its many special features that they insisted the contractor build the frame and rooms before the cement foundation was completely dry? Of course, the result would be disaster. The wet cement, capable of supporting thousands of pounds when dry, would not yet be able to support even a small amount. Walls would sink into the concrete, correct angles and dimensions would be impossible to maintain, and strength would be forfeited. Even after eventual drying, cracks and other problems would develop—the house would be unsafe to live in. What a waste. Because the couple could not wait to enjoy the house, they did not allow the foundation to dry properly. They themselves ruined their house. They cannot blame the contractor who warned them; they can blame only their own impatience. Now neither they nor anyone else will ever enjoy that house.

Similarly, single adults who are unwilling to be patient and put forth the effort to build a solid foundation for their relationships face an unsteady foundation. Eventually it will collapse. Even if God has brought them together and blessed them with enormous potential, they can destroy the finished product if they try to proceed too rapidly. This is true in many areas: couples can get too close, too soon emotionally, financially, and socially (premature commitments). However, the danger is most prevalent in the area of physical, sexual intimacy. In terms of the analogy, some couples try to move their bed into the house while the foundation is wet and before the walls are up.

THE HIDDEN OPPORTUNITY

In spite of the ways that sexuality can be abused before marriage, sexuality can be an asset if used in the appropriate way. Single sexuality can be seen as a gift of God, the very vehicle and motivation of the *imago Dei*. God has left the sexual switch for single adults in the "on" position for a purpose. Of course, God is taking a risk with us, but He feels we are worth it. God is trusting singles to understand and apply a healthy, theologically sound view of sexuality that is consistent both before and after marriage. We should recognize His intent for our attractions and desires, and use our desires wisely, as He intended. God desires that we see our impulses as blessings and yet not sin—as opportunities and yet not fall.

So what is the hidden opportunity in a single's sexuality? Simply this: *sexuality is God's reminder to the single adult to be wisely relational.* As singles find themselves physically attracted to others, they are to use that attraction as a reminder that God wants them to be develop quality relationships. To put it bluntly and in the first person, when I feel a sexual attraction for another person, I should grasp the opportunity and say to myself: *God is reminding me that He wants me to develop whole relationships, caring friendships.* This is the key to handling temptation, which we will discuss in the next chapter.

Questions for Discussion
1. Have you ever known someone who was afraid to love? Why was he or she that way?
2. Have you ever promised yourself that you would never trust men or women again? If so, when and why?
3. Read Romans 12:3–8. How does the idea of sexuality as a spiritual gift relate to those verses?
4. Have you ever been part of a close community and/or fellowship? What kind of group was it? What made it so close?
5. How does sexuality help us become whole people? What's the difference between a half-person and a whole person?
6. Have you ever known a couple that became too close, too soon? How did that affect their relationship?

CHAPTER EIGHT

HOW CAN I HANDLE TEMPTATION?

Here's a practical question. What should a single guy do when he is innocently walking down the street and all of the sudden a sexy woman, "dressed to kill," rounds the corner and walks straight towards him?

COMMON RESPONSES

Most single men who want to avoid lustful thoughts will try one of several options commonly used by singles: First, a single man can try to avoid looking at her. He can close his eyes and try to pretend he did not see her. One group of religious leaders in the time of Jesus believed that the only way to deal with sexual temptation was to close their eyes whenever they saw a beautiful woman. Unfortunately, some of them tried to keep walking, even with their eyes closed, and they would invariably run into buildings, walls, and other people, hurting themselves in the process. Thus they were called "the Blind and Bleeding Pharisees." Obviously, that was not a healthy way to deal with sexual temptation. In fact, it was not even helpful. As anyone who has seen something and then tries to turn away knows, it is almost impossible to get the image out of one's head.

Another common response for the man is anger and self-incrimination. A Christian man who has been taught that all such thoughts and desires are evil will become angry with himself for noticing her body and being sexually attracted. Some sincere singles will even begin to punish themselves for being attracted. When confronted with a sexual temptation, one man was so disappointed with himself that he would instantly launch into stream of verbal self-abuse. "You're such a scum, Chuck. There you go again. Why can't you control yourself? Others think you are a spiritual leader, but you can't even guard your own thoughts. What a fake. What an impostor . . . " He began to beat himself up with negative self-talk. After a bit of this type of self-mortification, he would feel a little better. This was because his abuse was a form of self-inflicted punishment. He felt that if he punished himself, then God wouldn't have to punish him later.

There are other options available, and women use them too. One devoted Christian woman whenever tempted to lust after an attractive man would feel condemned by God. She would say to herself, *There you go again, Sheila. Oh, God, I'm so sorry. You must be really disappointed in me. I must be a failure in your eyes. Please forgive me.* In spite of her many appeals for forgiveness, she had a hard time feeling forgiven. This was because she would be tempted again and again, and she believed that anyone who committed the same sin over and over was not truly repentant.

TEMPTATION IS NOT SIN

In all three instances, the common mistake was to assume that if a person is tempted sexually, he or she has given in to sin. But to be in a tempting situation does not mean that sin has occurred. There is a difference between temptation and acting on that temptation. Again, James 1:13–15 is very helpful:

> When tempted, no one should say, 'God is tempting me.' For God cannot be tempted by evil, nor does he tempt anyone; but each one is tempted when, by his own evil desire, he is dragged away and enticed. Then, after desire has conceived, it gives birth to sin; and sin, when it is full-grown, gives birth to death."

The difference between a tempting situation and a sinful situation is described by James as a process. First, there is the specific situation, and then there is the enticement to act on the temptation it presents, acting either mentally or physically. Finally, the temptation is acted out, and sin appears (is given "birth"). But notice carefully, there seems to be some type of moral space between enticement and the conception of sin. In other words, there is a difference between feeling enticed and allowing that enticement to give birth to a sinful act or thought.

Jesus describes a similar process in Matthew 5:27–28: "You have heard that it was said, 'Do not commit adultery.' But I tell you that anyone who looks at a woman lustfully has already committed adultery with her in his heart." In His subtle wisdom, Jesus does not say that to look upon a woman is to commit adultery; what is wrong is to look lustfully upon someone. There again seems to be a type of moral space between the innocent look and the lustful thought. The look, in and of itself, is not wrong. There is nothing inherently evil about seeing another person. It is what we do with this image that can give birth to sin. It must be possible, then, to look without lusting.

This applies directly to singles and situations of sexual temptation. To use our example again, when that single guy walks down the street and sees a sexually attractive woman, he is confronted with a temptation. He then has two additional choices: he can indulge that temptation or have victory over it. But a temptation is not the same thing as sin. If he indulges the temptation and allows it to fester in his mind by playing out a lustful scenario, then he has sinned. But if he refuses to engage the temptation, he can actually use that situation as a motivation to develop better relationships.

ONE SOLUTION: RELATIONAL PRAYER

How can he use a potentially damaging situation to develop godly relationships? My suggestion is this: Use the attraction as a reminder that God has created you to be a relational person, and make it just one more opportunity to commit yourself to developing personal wholeness and whole relationships.

When this happens to me, rather than staring at the woman (or billboard, or TV commercial, or whatever), I glance up to the heavens and offer up a prayer like this: *I thank you, God, for this reminder that you created me to be a relational person. I recommit myself here and now to developing whole, godly relationships that reflect Your image. Because of that, I will not engage my mind with this picture. Instead, dear Lord, I pray for those other, quality relationships that I am now working on. First I pray for my friendship with——(blank) . . . "*

Speaking as a man who was single until thirty years of age, I can personally testify as to the helpfulness of this approach. I was able to confront tempting situations and not be overwhelmed or drawn into undesirable thoughts. I would pray for my closest friends, for each of my family, for church friends, for new friends, for co-workers, and for non-Christian friends. And, of course, I would especially pray for the woman I was romantically interested in or involved with.

In addition, this approach greatly improved my prayer life. By using the tempting situations as calls to prayer, I would find myself drawn into prayer several times a day.

By the time I went through this mental prayer list, several things occurred. First, I felt a deeper love and positive regard for my friends. I found that even though my friends were not physically present, I was nonetheless able to work on our relationships. I could pray for them and God's blessing on their lives, and I concentrated on thanking God for the blessing of their friendships.

Second, I was able to do something positive for them—pray for their specific needs. Then the next time I was with my friends, I was honestly able to say, "I've been praying for you," or, "It's so good to see you. I've been thinking about you a lot and praying for———." I'll bet they thought I was some prayer warrior, spending hours a day on my knees in prayer. No, I was just a young man with normal hormones who lived in a sexually tempting culture. But each time I was tempted, I used that as a call to pray, and I prayed a lot!

Third, I was able to deal with my own weak spots. Whenever I pray for friends, there are always a few with whom I am feeling tension at present. Maybe I'm mad at a friend for an unkind thing she said. Maybe a friend is mad at me for a thoughtless gesture of my own. Maybe the friendship is experiencing growth pains as the two of us are drifting apart. Maybe I'm jealous of the attention my friend is receiving from others. There really are a hundred things that can cause irritations between friends. I try to pray about those irritants and allow God to prune me into the friend He wants me to be.

Finally, when I answer this unique call to prayer, I am strengthened in my own resolve to be a godly man of integrity and purity. This not only means that I do not want to allow a tempting situation to entice me into sin but also that I will not degrade others by using them as objects for my selfish desire.

A CALL TO PRAYER

Whether we are facing major temptations and crises or are simply proceeding through the pressures of the day, prayer empowers us. This concept of a call to prayer is not unusual. In a monastery or convent, the church bells will ring several times a day, calling the monks or nuns to gather for times of prayer. In the religion of Islam, devotees are called to prayer five times a day. At each appointed hour, Muslims are to face Mecca, kneel, and pray. In the time of Jesus, the Jewish leaders had developed a regular call to prayer. Jesus refers to this in

Matthew 6:6–15 when He says, "And when you pray . . . " He then takes their normal customs of prayer and corrects their abuses, but what He does not do is suggest that they abandon their calls to prayer. He assumes the opposite—that they will continue to pray regularly. Peter and John, two of the apostles, continued to follow this Jewish call to prayer, as is seen in Acts 3:1: "One day Peter and John were going up to the temple at the time of prayer at three in the afternoon."

In the Old Testament, court officials encouraged King Darius of Persia to issue a royal decree prohibiting normal prayer. They suggested to the king, "Anyone who prays to any god or man during the next thirty days, except to you, O king, shall be thrown into the lions' den" (Daniel 6:7). The officials knew that Daniel prayed to God three times a day, and they were jealous of him and his favor with the king.

The Scriptures record Daniel's brave response: "Now when Daniel learned that the decree had been published, he went home to his upstairs room where the windows opened toward Jerusalem. Three times a day he got down on his knees and prayed, giving thanks to God, just as he had done before" (Daniel 6:10). In spite of the king's edict, Daniel did not abandon his regular call to prayer.

To be sure, specific hours for prayer and tolling bells seem to be natural and appropriate calls to prayer. They even sound religious. But this idea of a sexually tempting situation as a call to prayer—well, that's quite different, I admit. However, I have found that God is not limited to the religious or sacred situations. He uses very normal people, things, and events to carry out His will. And the same is true with prayer. He uses common things to call us to prayer, if we will only be discerning enough to hear His voice. In fact, everything we see, hear, or do can be a call to prayer. If we see a person in need, read about a family tragedy in the newspaper, watch a news clip about an important diplomatic meeting—all of these things and more can be calls to prayer. In this way, we can easily live out what Paul suggested, "Pray without ceasing" (1 Thessalonians 5:17)

This concept is easy to misunderstand, so allow me to clarify what I don't mean by suggesting that temptation is a call to prayer. I'm not saying that the solution to temptation is the trite "Just pray about it." This would be no different that the earlier example of the man who avoided his sexuality by studying the Bible more. Neither am I suggesting that prayer will keep a person from sinning. Prayer is not a miracle cure. As we all know, it is possible to sin while praying (have you ever had an evil thought that kept creeping back into your mind during prayer?), and it is possible to pray while sinning. (Have you ever asked for forgiveness during the very moment of sin? Have you ever prayed,

"Oh, God, I know I shouldn't be doing this. Please forgive me.") A call to prayer is not a simplistic solution, it is not a guarantee, and it must not be used as a magic formula to insulate ourselves against temptation.

Instead, it is an effort to include God in the very details of life that seem most ungodly. This may seem simple, but it is not simplistic. The Christian life should not be compartmentalized. We humans are especially adept at dividing up our lives into different parts and then revealing those parts only when they seem appropriate. Children are especially good at this and are able to segment their language, mannerisms, and attitudes. For instance, children often have one vocabulary around mom and dad and a completely different one with their peers. Their parents are separated from a part of their children's experiences and personality. Some parents even like this—they claim to not want to know what goes on at school.

But God does not want to be allowed into only certain areas of our lives. He desires to be included in everything, not just those certain thoughts and actions that are clean and pure. The Bible says that God "never leaves us or forsakes us" (Hebrews 13:5), and that as our shepherd, the Lord walks with us even through the valley of the shadow of death (Psalm 23:4). This is one of God's most amazing attributes—His willingness to descend with us even to the depths of our depravity. The psalmist wrote, "If I make my bed in hell . . . even there your right hand will hold me" (Psalm 139:8, 10). About this verse Smedes commented, "If you fall into hell, you may land in the hand of God."[1]

A call to prayer during temptation is God's call to us to not exclude Him, to not shut the door in His face. He wants us to include Him at all times. That's why the summons to prayer originates from God, not within ourselves. Yes, I believe God uses temptation to call us to prayer. But by prayer I mean more than just the motions and verbage. He is doing something much more intimate and loving: He is sharing His desire for communication and relational interaction. In other words, He is reminding us to be in relationship with Him.

When I come home in the evening, my daughter usually runs to the door, jumps into my arms, and begins to tell me about her day. I just love it when she does that. But some days she is preoccupied or troubled, and the troubles seem to cause her to forget that I want to be involved with her. So if she doesn't come running, I go looking for her. I run after her and get involved in whatever she is doing, because I want to be a part of her life. I find her, kiss her, and ask what she's doing. Then she begins to tell me about her project, problem, or whatever. And I love that just as much. I don't care what we talk about, as long as we talk. I just want to communicate and relate with her.

Of course, we don't call our father/daughter discussions prayer. It's just talk. But since prayer is simply talk between a person and God, the analogy fits well. God welcomes our conversations with Him. And He cares as much about our interacting with Him as the content of the prayer. He is interested in our lives, ready to help during the tough times. And when we fail to go to God in prayer, He too will seek us out and call us into conversation. When Paul suggested to the Philippians "Don't worry about anything; instead, pray about everything" (Philippians 4:6 TLB*), he wasn't merely suggesting, "Just pray about it." He was calling them to something much deeper, an open and ongoing relationship with God. In essence, he was saying that they should include God in every facet of their lives. That's how we can pray without ceasing.

During such moments of fellowship and conversation with God, He will aid us by leading us to other resources to help us in our battles—the strength of His Word, accountability of fellowship, and the value of self-discipline. All of these will become valuable weapons in the fight against temptation and will help us to respond to temptation by resisting it, fleeing it, and denying it any power over our lives.

This idea of sensing God's call to prayer during a sexually tempting occasion helped me transform a potentially destructive situation into a positive experience. This is what James meant when he instructed Christians, "Consider it pure joy, my brothers, whenever you face trials of many kinds, because you know that your faith develops perseverance. Perseverance must finish its work so that you may be mature and complete, not lacking in anything" (James 1:2–4).

J. B. Phillips captured the essence of turning every temptation to good in this translation of the above verses:

> When all kinds of trials and temptations crowd into your lives, my brothers, don't resent them as intruders, but welcome them as friends! Realise that they come to test your faith and to produce in you the quality of endurance. But let the process go on until that endurance is fully developed, and you will find you have become men of mature character with the right sort of independence.

As a single adult, I slowly learned how to welcome instances of temptation—even sexual temptation—as friends rather than enemies. They were like spiritual advisers that reminded me to stay in relationship with God, to keep developing wholeness and intimacy with Him

* The Living Bible.

and others. And now that I am married, this still continues to work very well. After all, the tempting situations do not cease after the proverbial knot is tied. I still use such situations as a call to prayer, but now the prayer has changed slightly:

"Thank you, dear God, for loving and blessing me so much! And thank you for this reminder that you want me to be a relational man, working hard to develop the kind of marriage, family, and friendships that reflect your glory. I first of all thank you for my wonderful wife, Amy . . ."

GOD'S REMINDERS

It may sound strange, but any tempting situation can become an enriching moment if we recognize within it a hidden call to prayer. In this way, sexual power will be used for godly ends, and its strength can be channeled into developing quality Christian relationships. The urges that draw us toward others will not be denied or avoided but will be taken as signals from God. They are God's reminders to us that we are not to give up on relationships with others, even though the pain of past relationships has made us gun-shy. God will not allow us to remove ourselves from relationships and become hermetic outcasts. He will not passively watch us diminish the glory of His image in us. Love is too important; intimacy is too central to who and what we are.

Our sexuality is God's reminder to us that we are to work toward developing friendships. At each stirring of sexuality within us, He is gently telling us again that we were created to be relational people. Seen from this perspective, our sexual urges become positive reminders, and the energy can be used to advance toward healthy and Christian goals. The impulses become opportunities for obedience rather than temptations toward sin.

THE DEEPEST REASON

Though our sexuality is how God's ensures we we will be involved in relationships, this is not the main reason God has made sexuality an integral part of our being. After all, even our earthly friendships and loves are only preludes to the most delightful music to come. What is this music? John gives us the answer: "We proclaim to you what we have seen and heard, so that you also may have fellowship with us. And our fellowship is with the Father and with His Son, Jesus Christ. We write this to make our joy complete" (1 John 1:3–4).

Here is the ultimate purpose of human relationships, the deepest reason that God leaves our sex switches on: human love is a laboratory in which we develop our ability to relate with and love *God* in a complete, full way. Rather than just creating humans and plopping us into heavenly bliss, God in His wisdom chose to let us grow to value and appreciate intimacy first here on earth. As Paul described in the beautiful love chapter, 1 Corinthians 13, we are only able to love imperfectly as humans. He writes, "Now we see but a poor reflection as in a mirror; then we shall see face to face. Now I know in part; then I shall know fully, even as I am fully known" (1 Corinthians 13:12). Love between humans is imperfect, imprecise, impeded.

Such obstacles to perfect love we cannot remove. They are barriers that cannot be surmounted or broken through. This does not mean that earthly love is valueless, though. It is of immense value and worth, both in its own right and as a kind of tutor. In Greek days, a tutor was called a *pedagogos,* from *paidos,* "a young boy," and *agogos,* "to lead." Thus a pedagogos was a leader or teacher of young children. Even today, a schoolteacher sometimes takes special effort to tutor the little informed. Earthly love, then, is an instructor for us, a tutor in the ways of relationship and intimacy. We learn what true love is and is not. We discover the value of deep, enduring intimacy, and we grow in our own ability to experience and appreciate love.

We are like little children who are created with an ear to enjoy the best of philharmonic music. But our wise teacher knows that if we attend the best symphony without any instruction or experience, we probably will neither appreciate nor enjoy the music fully. So before we are ever allowed to go to a symphony, the teacher first takes us to a practice room, pulls out instruments, and begins to teach us how to make music ourselves. Of course, the instruments are old and worn, and even at our best the music is marginal. At first, it is fun to learn how to play the different instruments; it's sort of a game. But soon we realize that making beautiful music is no game—it's serious business and requires effort and concentration.

More than that, we soon discover that playing well is the result of countless hours of practice and sacrifice. Several children decide that music isn't worth the effort, and they abandon the music room for the monkey bars and swings. But a few of us remain in the room. Why do we remain? Because we have begun to discover the wonder and joy of music.

Finally, the big day of the field trip to the symphony arrives. We all board the bus, even the ones who chose to play on the bars and swings.

Of course, those of us who chose to leave our instruments for the bars and swings find the concert kind of boring. We fidget and shift in our seats a lot. The reason? We have not learned how to love music. But for those of us who kept practicing, the concert exceeds even our grandest expectations. The conductor is masterful, the musicians incredible, the instruments beautiful, and the auditorium magnificent. But best of all is the music—what wonderful, grand music! In our wildest dreams we never imagined music sounding so sweet. That's what heaven will be like for those who are willing to learn the lessons of love here on earth. The joys will be deeper, the music sweeter, and—most important—the intimacy with God more valued and appreciated. In addition, the reunion with our friends and loved ones—and, I believe, the new friendships we will make there—will be richer and more fulfilling. What began here on earth in relationships with others and with God will find its ultimate completion in what the Bible calls the New Jerusalem. Heaven is not a place of boredom, filled only with harps and clouds. And it is not a carnival or theme park, catering to every whim, passion, and excitement. Heaven is a place in which the intimacy we were created to reflect will find its true fulfillment. There the image of God within us will shine in full glory. Heaven, to put it in a nutshell, will be "Friendshipland."

Such a place is hard for us to even imagine, since here on earth friendships are fragile and problematic. But finally, our innate desire to love and be loved will be completely satisfied both by intimacy with God and with other lovers of God. This is what the Bible tries to convey in its language about eternal life with God. The Revelation's grand description of heaven has much to say about the quality of our relationships there:

> Then I saw a new heaven and a new earth, for the first heaven and the first earth had passed away, and there was no longer any sea. I saw the Holy City, the new Jerusalem, coming down out of heaven from God, prepared as a bride beautifully dressed for her husband. And I heard a loud voice from the throne saying, "Now the dwelling of God is with men, and he will live with them. They will be his people, and God himself will be with them and be their God. He will wipe every tear from their eyes. There will be no more death or mourning or crying or pain, for the old order of things has passed away."
>
> He who was seated on the throne said, "I am making everything new!" Then he said, "Write this down, for these words are trustworthy and true."
>
> He said to me: "It is done. I am the Alpha and the Omega, the Beginning and the End. To him who is thirsty I will give to drink without cost from the spring of the water of life. He who overcomes will inherit all this, and I will be his God and he will be my son." (Rev. 21:1–7)

IS CELIBACY ENOUGH?

If our sexuality is God's training ground here for the richness of interpersonal relationships in heaven, that need not imply it is of no earthly good. Earthly sexuality can be a great thing in and of itself—if it is approached from the perspective of value. But the heavenly realities also point to another benefit. By locating sexuality in the context of spiritual matters, we are reminded that sex is important to God. Even more, it is essential to understand that true sexual and interpersonal fulfillment will only develop in the context of a healthy relationship with God.

Thus the deeper reason for our sexuality also sheds light on the way singles can begin to recover a sense of purity and self-worth in this life. In the daily experience of God's love and forgiveness we learn how to love and forgive ourselves.

A SINGLE SPEAKS

I was one who in my early twenties thought that I was "technically" a virgin, not realizing that sex was a lot more than intercourse. I wish someone had told me then. I was briefly involved in intercourse with a boyfriend—the only one I was ever involved with. I decided I no longer wanted to be sexually active, stopped, and eventually we broke up; he married.

I have been celibate for about thirteen years now, but I didn't feel pure and white as snow. Why not? Surely I have confessed this enough and know intellectually what God can do and that He can make me pure. But I realized that there was no man in my life to make me feel valuable and cherished, so in my heart of hearts I didn't feel that. I still felt second class, like a reject. I also realize that men (the human beings that they are) are imperfect and not going to love us women as we need and desire or that my needs might be so great that no human being could ever meet them—only one relationship can, the relationship with Jesus.

I realized that in order to feel pure again, I needed to sense the value and cherishing that Jesus feels toward me. I need to sense His deep love for me. I can only do that by "diving deep" into a relationship with Him—getting deep in prayer and in His Word, reading about His love for me and allowing myself to sense that love. I see no other way to feel pure again; just being celibate didn't do it for me. It's probably been seven years since I've even kissed a man, though I have dated.

This single woman has grasped fully the concepts of fulfillment and value. She understands that celibacy is only one part of the journey towards personal wholeness, self-worth, and a recovered purity. Another necessary ingredient is a deeply personal experience of God's presence, love, and forgiveness.

Questions for Discussion

1. Can intimacy be developed between two singles without any sexual activity?

2. Look at Matthew 5:27–30 and James 1:13–15. Do you think that these Scriptures suggest that the physical urges themselves are sinful, or that one's response to his or her sexual urges can bring about sin?

3. Is working on relationships much of a priority in your life? Why or why not? Give specific examples to illustrate your answer.

4. Do you agree that sexually tempting situations can become "calls to prayer"? Consider those situations that are most tempting for you. How could you pray on those occasions? Write out a sample prayer—it may come in handy soon!

5. This chapter claimed that human intimacy helps us develop intimacy with God. How do you feel about your relationship with God at this point in your life? Why?

PART THREE
HOW FAR IS TOO FAR?

CHAPTER NINE

SHOULD SEXUAL INTIMACY INCREASE WITH COMMITMENT?

How far is too far?" At least one brave person asks that bottom-line question whenever I speak about sexual relationships.

A man, thinking through the concepts yet still wanting an easy answer, asked, "How much can we get away with and still communicate value?" From a different motivational perspective, a woman asked, "What things can we do sexually and not get God mad at us?" Her question revealed to me that she really hadn't caught the major concept of sexuality as a way of protecting and asserting value.

"How far can we go and stay within God's limits?" another single asked on a card anonymously. "Are kissing, petting, holding hands, oral sex, and/or nudity permissible for Christians who are trying to abstain from intercourse before marriage?" Now, that's an honest, direct question.

THE IMPORTANCE OF VALUE

Before answering specifically, I'd like to once again repeat the two major theses of this book: sexual celibacy is a way of protecting and asserting personal worth and value, and the sex drive is God's way of motivating us to keep working on personal wholeness and interpersonal intimacy. Therefore, in order to decide how "far" two unmarried people should proceed sexually, the deciding factor will be our key word, *value*. We must ask ourselves, "How do the specific acts affect my sense of personal worth and value?" Therefore, the bottom-line answer to the question, "How far is too far?" is simple: *Engage only in those physical expressions that protect and assert mutual value.*

What does that mean? The heart of the matter is not what singles can get away with. Instead, the issue is how sexual expression communicates and builds up a personal sense of value. But before we consider how we can build a sense of value through our sexual expression, let's hear from a couple of singles who illustrate that a person doesn't have to go "all the way" to feel devalued.

Sarah remained a virgin yet felt devalued before marriage. As she describes her relationship, "I look back to my past and although I did not have premarital sex, I can remember feeling used and 'de-valued.' At the time, I thought it was *my* problem since we were not going 'all the way.' Even today in my marriage, I still feel the pain from not asserting my own needs and sensitivities but trying (unsuccessfully) to please my husband. While this is changing, I realize that there are still areas where I am not totally honest with myself and my husband."

In "A Single Speaks," read about a woman who felt greatly devalued in her relationship even though she remained technically a virgin. She had strong, positive instruction from her church leaders, yet still felt devalued because of certain sexual activities.

A SINGLE SPEAKS

I grew up in a medical household where things were explained meticulously and without embarrassment. I recall asking my parents where the neighbor's dog got her puppies, and it was at that moment I received my reproductive lecture. My parents tell me that I was bored by their explanation and went outside to play after they were done, without asking questions.

It was in fifth grade when my first formal sex education took place in the school system, and I remember already being aware of all the information that was presented. In eighth grade there was another sex education unit, and this time I remember being more interested in the material. Issues of birth control and sexually transmitted diseases were addressed, and this became a controversial issue in the school system.

In terms of my education outside the school system and outside of the home, I really applaud the junior high and high school leaders at my church. Several Sunday nights were spent addressing the issues involved in sexuality, most especially the reality of desire in the adolescent. In looking back at my youth leaders, I believe they operated in the framework of value, respect, and gentle guidance, not condemnation with a list of don'ts. I continue today to be impacted by their healthy model of sexuality in a Christian context.

Aside from my educational experience in sexuality, I have minimal experience in the context of relationships. I am single and in my early twenties and currently not involved in what anyone would call a serious relationship. I remember my first real kiss was in the fifth grade when my boyfriend kissed me on the playground. I remember thinking it was funny but that I was also afraid. I then remember playing spin-the-bottle at boy-girl parties in junior high and kissing my junior high dance dates.

My experiences in junior high and then in high school included flirting, holding hands, hugging, and kissing. In high school the paradigm began to change when some of my friends started to have sex. It was at this point that I was very involved in church, and I did not feel pressured, but I was very intrigued by the experiences of my friends. I went to a very large high school and was in a very popular crowd that lots of kids envied. It was in my senior year that I felt pressure to get some more experience. I didn't want to have sex, but I felt that I needed more experience.

One of my best friends in high school had parents that were away every weekend, and we had parties at her house, especially in the hot tub. It was one night after a football game when I was in the hot tub with a guy I liked, but didn't know well, and engaged in heavy petting.

The next morning I felt disgusting. I actually threw up because I had done that, and my friends could not believe I was so upset. They kept telling me I was a nice innocent person and should not feel guilty. I was dramatically affected by this experience. I could not even face this guy in school, and when he gave a party, I didn't want to go. He was so nice and felt horrible that I was so upset. Ultimately I had betrayed my own belief system and felt that I had devalued myself. From that point on, I did not put myself in those kinds of situations. I graduated from high school, went off to college, and had dates to all my sorority events but did not date anyone seriously.

As the stories of Sarah and our other single person illustrate, the issue of "how far can singles go?" is not as simple as it may first seem. Though neither of these singles had premarital sexual intercourse, they both claim to have been devalued by sexual expression other than intercourse. What these singles have to teach us is that it is not direct intercourse alone that can make a single feel devalued. Any sexual activity, if engaged in prematurely, can be injurious. That's why it's crucial that singles have a clear idea about what to do and what not to do in dating.

In search of the answer to these questions, singles flock to Christian bookstores, seminars, and counseling sessions, hoping to find a clear, ethical model to help them navigate these risky storms. The answers are as diverse as they are confusing, ranging from "Don't do anything at all" to "Anything goes." But again, what singles need is not a list of dos and don'ts; they aren't helped in the long run by a rule book that's supposed to guide their behavior. What singles really need is *a sensible model* with which they can make their own, informed decisions about how far is too far. My appeal in this book is for a new model, a sexual ethic for singles based on *value* and *commitment.*

AN INADEQUATE MODEL:
THE SINGLES' SEX TRIANGLE

The idea of a sexual ethic based on commitment, of course, is not new. For many years, respected Christian authors, counselors, and professors have been teaching what I call "the singles' sex triangle" as a practical guideline for Christian singles. This popular model is helpful yet incomplete, even though it is probably the most popular ethic for singles and sexuality today. We will explore its weaknesses shortly, but first let's acknowledge its benefits and its advocates.

The singles' sex triangle remains the dominant model, and it certainly is in vogue in Christian academia. In fact, recently I attended a panel discussion on singles and sexuality at an evangelical seminary, where the professors in the counseling department presented the triangle with enthusiasm. In my early years in singles ministry, I too felt this was the best model available and taught it to a few singles groups. But with each presentation, I discovered more and more flaws within the argument and finally abandoned it after I was able to pinpoint the missing element.

Simply put, this ethic teaches that the levels of physical involvement and commitment should be equal. As the level of commitment rises, so too should the amount of physical intimacy. This is best illustrated by a triangle, in which one leg represents the physical side of a relationship, and the other represents the commitment side. The apex of the triangle is marriage, at which time sexual intercourse is said to be appropriate.

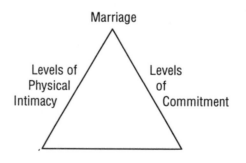

The triangle implies a progression of involvement. As two singles grow closer and closer in their relationship and move towards marriage, this should be reflected in a gradual and yet commensurate rise in both their sexual intimacy and in their commitment to exclusivity. For example, let's imagine that two singles named Roy and Barbara meet and decide to date. On their first date, the singles sex triangle would teach that both physical intimacy and commitments should be kept minimal. The couple should engage only in small levels of physical expression to correspond to the fact that they do not share any strong commitments to each other. As their dating life progresses and their love and commitment to each other grows, so too their life together can be gradually and safely built. In our diagram, this progression looks like successive layers of an Egyptian pyramid.

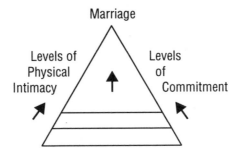

This is the picture of a balanced sex triangle. However, if Roy and Barbara were to become so enraptured that they jumped in the sack on that first date, they would throw the triangle terribly out of balance, putting the future health of their blossoming relationship in danger. To get too close too soon physically puts an enormous strain on a relationship. It's difficult to keep everything in perspective and balance when one side is wildly out of proportion.

To switch metaphors momentarily, relationships are like cargo ships. If a ship is loaded carefully and properly, it can carry enormous weights and perform terrific tasks. But if the ship is loaded improperly, the whole thing will sink. This is especially obvious in an extreme situation: if the crew tried to fully load only one side of the ship while leaving the other side almost empty, disaster would result. Even if they recognized the problem and tried quickly to put more cargo on the empty side, in most cases it would be too late. The ship would capsize.

That's what happens to couples who load their budding relationship with too much on one side, while the other side remains empty. In terms of the singles' sex triangle model, their imbalanced relationship, which emphasizes physical intimacy too soon, looks something like the triangle below, left.

But danger lurks not only on the physical side. A couple can also become out of balance by committing themselves too quickly. If Roy and Barbara became deeply infatuated that first night and in the throes of infatuation decided to get married, the singles sex triangle again would be out of balance, as shown below, right.

Out-of-Balance Relationships

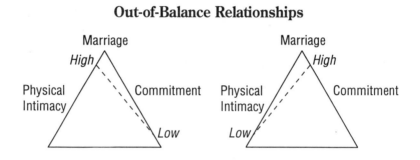

The singles' sex triangle is an illustration that is clear, sensible, and easy to apply. Its genius, and why it has been so popular among Christian educators and teachers, is its ability to give singles a reason to slow down their drive for sexual intimacy—it gives singles a clear reason for not hopping in the sack at any time. In addition, the singles' sex triangle has helped singles understand that developing intimacy is a process; to build a high-quality, lasting relationship takes time and balance.

This view appeared in print first in 1971 in the small book *I Married You*, by Walter Trobisch. *I Married You* was targeted not only for married couples but also for those contemplating marriage or already engaged. The triangles drawn by Trobisch were slightly different, but the message was the same. This illustration was a powerful educational tool for Trobisch in his work in Africa and helped him convince his unmarried parishioners not to rush into sexual intimacy. One of his students took readily to the illustration and commented on how he saw this played out in the lives of other young Africans:

> What usually happens is this: The young man says to the girl, "I love you," and what he means is just an inch in the direction of faithfulness. But the girl is so happy about it that she, in turn, allows him to go three inches in the direction of intimacy.

Then the boy thinks, *This worked fine,* so he adds another inch toward faithfulness. The girl replies by giving him four more inches in the direction of intimacy. Before they know it, they end up at the sex angle, without being about to carry the full responsibility for this step. Instead of parallel lines you then have slanted lines.[1]

A more recent exposition of the singles' sex triangle can be found in Richard Foster's *Money, Sex, and Power.* This 1985 book was his insightful, contemporary application of the three traditional monastic vows of poverty, celibacy, and obedience to the current issues of money, sex, and power. In his chapter "Sexuality and Singles," Foster deals with the important issues of fantasies, masturbation, and the single life.[2]

Foster give a clear definition of what we have called the singles' sex triangle: "Increased physical intimacy in a relationship should always be matched by increased commitment to that relationship."[3] Thomas Jones recommends Foster's approach as a healthy one and does not see the problems inherent nor the inconsistencies in his suggested guidelines. Jones says, "The morality of petting depends entirely upon the nature and depth of the relationship between two people. . . . The only dependable method to measure the strength of a relationship is to ask what kind of promises, or commitments, the two people are willing to give to each other"[4]

Seminary professor Lewis Smedes in his groundbreaking book *Sex for Christians* also endorses the triangle model. He describes how this approach affects one form of physical expression, "petting," or caressing: "Petting is a halfway house between shunning all physical expressions on the one hand, and rushing swiftly toward sexual intercourse on the other. But petting can also be a one-tenth or nine-tenths of the way home. The deeper and closer to commitment the personal relationship is, the more heavy the petting *properly becomes*"[5] (italics added).

PROBLEMS WITH THIS GEOMETRY

There are several serious problems with this approach. What is meant by petting? What constitutes "light" physical intimacy versus "heavy" intimacy may be different to different people, and the physical responses triggered also may be different.

Clearly individuals will view the allowable levels of physical intimacy differently. Out of curiosity I once asked an entire singles group to fill out the singles' sex triangle anonymously, noting only their gender. On the physical intimacy side, I wrote the words, in ascending order:

kiss, caress, disrobe, and *intercourse.* They were to put on the commitment side what they felt an appropriate stage for each action was. As you might have guessed, even though they were all active members of a Christian singles group, their responses came back quite varied. One surprise to me was that the gender did not make a difference—both women and men gave a large variety of answers.

Of course, most of them were pretty conservative. One woman's response matched that of about half of the group:

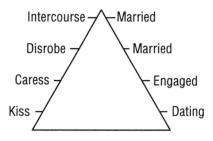

Several men gave responses that were even more traditional:

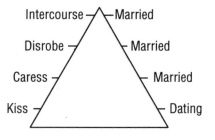

Others' responses were not so conservative, to say the least. One woman gave an interesting response:

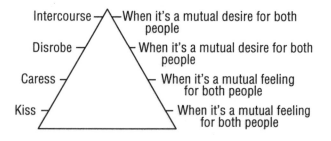

This women distinguished between "a mutual feeling" and a "mutual desire." To be honest, I have no idea what the difference might be between having a mutual feeling and a mutual desire, but I guess she believed it was important enough to distinguish between keeping her clothes on or not. Another woman had a much more specific time line for when certain physical intimacies were appropriate:

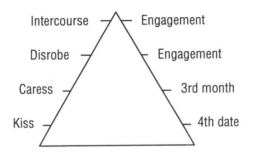

Similarly, a man was able to get quite specific:

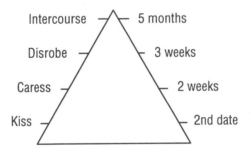

Now if I were dating someone with this view, I would want to know early in the relationship! In the same way, I would want to be aware of the following woman's shugles' sex triangle:

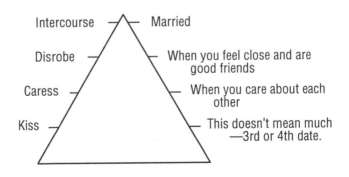

This last response is full of problems. It's good that she reserved intercourse for marriage, but I consider it strange that she disrobes whenever she feels close and the person is a good friend. Does that mean she disrobes with lots of friends? And how is it different from her answer to caressing—does she care about people and sexually caress them without feeling close to them or being good friends? Finally, what is the difference between dating and caring for someone? Does she date people she doesn't care for? I guess the saddest part is the little statement that kisses don't mean much.

It sounds to me as if she has been treated cheaply for so long that she has come to forget that kisses can be a valuable expression between two people. Her logic is confusing, to say the least. She is like a ship without a compass. Frankly, I wonder if she ever says no to anyone who wants her sexually.

Though she is certainly responsible for her actions, in one sense she could also be perceived as a victim. The loss of moral guidelines in our culture has left people in this bankrupt state, unable to make informed moral decisions. This is especially evident in the final triangle, done again by a woman:

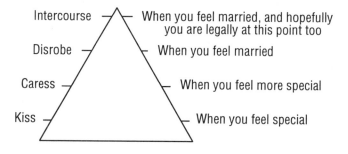

ENGAGEMENT AND COMMITMENT

The previous five triangles suggest that increasing commitment can result in complete physical intimacy. Thus engagement becomes grounds for heavy sexual involvement. Indeed, many Christians believe that withholding physical intimacy during engagement is unnecessary. After all, a commitment has been given with a ring, and it is likely there has been a public announcement of engagement. Those who think sexual union during engagement is acceptable typically accept the faulty biblical interpretations of a pastor or a youth pastor, or of misinformed friends.

Sadly, the idea of commitment being sufficient for physical union is being taught in some of today's most conservative, Christian colleges and by some evangelical ministers. Listen to one woman's account of such an ethic—and her resultant rationalization:

> In October of my senior year I met my [future] husband. We met at my Halloween party, and he called me two days later for a date. Well, I had never been on a true date, so, being the shy person I am, I asked if I could cook dinner for him. He was hooked. After two weeks of dating we were kissing and heavy petting. We began sleeping together (no sex). We had told each other we loved each other many times by this point. In December we talked about marriage and decided to make that commitment. We made love for the first time three months after we met. I never felt devalued. In fact, our pastor that did our premarital counseling discussed what marriage meant to God. There never were any ceremonies or weddings. This means little to God. It is the commitment made between two people before God that is true marriage.
>
> Yes, Pastor Stedman, I do feel that in God's eyes we were married. Our pastor agrees. You may not, because you place value on a paper document and a ceremony. In biblical days a wedding consisted of the groom taking the bride into his tent and before God stating their commitment to one another and then consummating the marriage. It is important that before you preach your sermon on value that you find out what marriage means to each individual. Our marriage has been wonderful and our sex very intimate and strong. You may find yourself devaluing a person because their beliefs differ from yours. Be careful. You may try to fix someone that doesn't need fixing. It is important that you define your idea of marriage so that everyone understands where you are coming from.

Though this woman was obviously disturbed and angry at my presentation, I considered it an honor that she was willing to write to me these very honest and vulnerable thoughts. But her logic is a bit lacking in a few areas. First of all, though some couples in the Old Testament times did not go through elaborate marriage ceremonies, many did. In Genesis 29, Jacob agrees to serve Laban for seven years for the privilege of marrying his younger daughter, Rachel. At the end of the seven years, Jacob said to Laban, "Give me my wife. My time is completed, and I want to lie with her" (Genesis 29:21). Obviously, though the two were betrothed, they had no sexual relations until after the seven years and the completion of their marriage feast. There are many more examples in the Bible of couples refraining from a sexual relationship during their engagement, including Joseph and Mary, the mother of Jesus (Matthew 1:18–19).

Another mistake in this woman's letter was her appeal to her own feelings and the suggestion that I find out "what marriage means to each individual." As any ethicist knows, feelings are not a good basis for ethical judgments, and the meaning of marriage cannot be found by popular survey. From a Christian standpoint, it is not each person who defines what marriage is, but God Himself though the Scriptures. Finally, though she tried to relate her situation to an Old Testament custom, I doubt if she and her fiancé really made their commitment to marriage and their sexual consummation public knowledge, as those ancients did. Before taking anyone into a tent, they would make their commitments openly and publicly, and the whole community would know that they were physically consummating that public vow in private.

I am happy for this couple that, in time, things have worked out well. Unfortunately, other equally committed couples are not so fortunate and do feel devalued by sexual intimacy too soon. Listen to the equally honest account of Theresa, who was a leader at an evangelical college ministry:

> I always felt it was very important for the woman to be a woman and be pure sexually before marriage. But I had a friend that went to [a conservative Christian college] and told me that there she learned that if you had sex before marriage, but it was just with the man you would later marry, it was OK, because that's how they did it in Old Testament times. I no longer believe this to be true, but unfortunately this encouraged me to get sexually involved briefly with an old boyfriend years ago. I am sorry I believed her. That little bit of false teaching has caused me much pain over the years.
>
> Though I had read and heard a lot about the benefits of being celibate as a single, I really had lost the feeling (that I once possessed) that my celibacy and purity were of value.

Obviously, this idea that sex before marriage between engaged or committed couples has been destructive in the lives of many single adults. Sure, there are a few who sleep together before marriage and don't get hurt—just as there are some people who play Russian roulette and live to tell about it, and kids who play with fire and don't burn anything down. Once I even heard of a man whose parachute didn't open, and he lived to talk about it. In spite of his story, I wouldn't suggest that people should try to skydive without parachutes, play Russian roulette, or mess with fire. And just because the ancients had a certain social practices or because people in the Old Testament did things a certain way, it doesn't follow that we should uncritically adopt those measures today. If that were the case, those who commit adultery would have to be killed—and we would lose half of our adult population. From the comments above and a study of the singles sex triangle, it is clear that increasing physical intimacy can rob a person of value.

The triangle model clearly has problems, whether one is engaged or just beginning to date. It raises key questions about protecting our value as a person (and the value of our partner), questions we will discuss in the next chapter.

Questions for Discussion
1. The singles' sex triangle teaches that sexual intimacy should rise in proportion to the level of commitment. Have you ever heard this before? When? Where?
2. The first problem with the singles' sex triangle is the difficulty singles have with the different levels and the activities that match those levels. But this is all theory unless you fill in your own triangle. Think back to some relationships you have had and fill in the triangle for yourself and the other person. There is room on the next page to note at least three of your past relationships, but don't stop there if you have had more significant relationships. This exercise will help you view those relationships in an entirely new light.

My Single Triangles

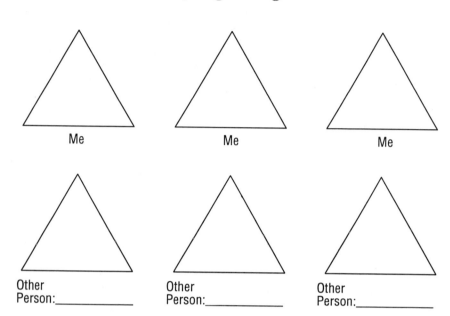

CHAPTER TEN

SHOULD SINGLES FEEL COMPELLED TO BE SEXUALLY INTIMATE?

hough the sex triangle helps many singles to postpone intercourse until marriage, it creates other problems. It actually encourages deeper and deeper sexual intimacy before marriage. The sex triangle requires that we keep our level of physical contact no higher than our level of commitment. But if the commitment is very high, say the second month of engagement or even three weeks until the wedding day, what happens to our physical intimacy?

PROBLEMS WITH THE TRIANGLE: LIMITS

The implication of the triangle model is that intimacy will be very high. The couple is told to refrain from intercourse, but most other forms of sexual intimacy seem approved, if this model is to be applied fully. Technically the couple may keep their virginity, but otherwise they are allowed to pursue sexual desires. Obviously one's value is threatened by this approach. But do we really want to teach singles that before marriage "anything goes" except intercourse?

I think that Richard Foster realized there were a few problems with the singles' sex triangle, even though he fully embraced this paradigm and suggested it to singles as a guide for behavior. He wrote,

> I have sought to present a general principle for responsible passion that I hope will provide guidance without legalism. I would like to add to this two opinions of my own. . . . My first suggestion

is this: since our purpose is to convey personal closeness and sharing without sexual intercourse, I think it would be wise to make the
genitals and the woman's breasts off limits until marriage. These
areas are just too explosive to be part of a mutual expression of
affection and caring short of intercourse.

My second suggestion is that the engagement period not be
too long—certainly not more than six months.[1]

Foster warns singles to avoid the touching of personal areas before marriage in order to avoid possible intercourse. However, if they
follow his triangle model, they would be *compelled* to disagree with his
suggestion. The logic of the singles' sex triangle actually propels a couple to engage in petting and genital intimacies before marriage.

I discovered this when a single man, who was a leader in his
church's singles ministry, spoke with me about a seminar on single sexuality that he and his fiancée attended. The speaker presented a ver-
sion of the singles' sex triangle, and he and his fiancée accepted it, in
his words, "hook, line, and sinker." Though they had been quite controlled sexually until that point, they believed that, in order to be
healthy, they should become more physically intimate! As a result, they
began to become sexually active to the point of mutual masturbation
and orgasm, but they were still committed to remain virgins until their
marriage. But in spite of their higher level of physical intimacy, they
were feeling that their relationship honored God less and less, and they
were feeling less and less qualified to be in Christian leadership.

"Rick, I try to convince myself that it's OK, but I would be totally
ashamed if anyone in the church found out about it!" this leader told
me. "I feel like such a hypocrite. I can't wait until we are married so I
can quit feeling so guilty about this."

PROBLEMS WITH THE TRIANGLE: PATIENCE

His impatience is reminiscent of another suggestion by propon-
ents of the model—that Christian engagements should not be longer
than six months. As Foster explains, "By the time a couple reaches the
point of engagement, they are entering levels of intimacy that should
not be sustained for long without expression in sexual intercourse."[2]

His timetable and conclusion are incorrect, for several reasons.
First, how does Foster derive the specific limit of "certainly not more
than six months"? The period is completely arbitrary.

Second, why does he believe that upon engagement, the couple
"are entering levels of intimacy that should not be sustained for long
without expression in sexual intercourse." It is because the logic of the

single's sex triangle naturally leads couples to get more physically involved once they are engaged.

Since engagement is high on the commitment scale, in order to
keep the model in balance, couples have to proceed to a corresponding-
ly high level of physical intimacy. This is why Foster recommends short
engagements. If the couple really follows the model, they will remain
virgins in a technical sense only. This development obviously was not a
comfortable one for Foster, so he felt compelled to add his own opinions to correct the model. Yet rather than helping, in doing so Foster
exposes the weakness inherent in the whole singles' sex triangles paradigm. In my mind, his suggestions are proof that the singles' sex triangle model is a poor one.

Third, his suggestion that engagements not be long reflects a low
view of the spirituality of Christian singles. One would imagine that
Foster would consider patience to be a necessary prerequisite for marriage, and the lack thereof not an excuse to hasten the marriage date.
This is all the more amazing because, from a historical point of view,
within monasticism the vow of celibacy was a means of teaching patience and self-discipline. As Foster himself says much earlier in the
book:

> The vow of chastity also witnesses against unrestrained self-indul-
> gence. It reminds us that discipline and denial are gospel impera-
> tives. You see, our sexual intoxication is only representative of an
> all-pervasive mood of intemperance that dominates the world in
> which we live today. The Franciscan Brother Giles once said, "By
> chastity I mean to keep guard over all the senses with the grace of
> God."[3]

Celibacy teaches patience. This is a lesson of value. We all could
benefit from a refresher course in self-discipline in this very basic area.
Maybe that's one reason the apostle Paul, when speaking about sexual
expression within marriage, recommends that Christian married couples, from time to time, abstain from sex for the purpose of prayer:
"Do not deprive each other except by mutual consent and for a time, so
that you may devote yourselves to prayer" (1 Corinthians 7:5). How
can abstinence add to one's prayer life?

Temporary celibacy, Paul is suggesting, would be a sort of fasting. It is well known that the effectiveness and pathos of prayer is increased when accompanied by fasting from food. But food is not the
only thing from which we can fast. As I heard Foster teach once in an
excellent sermon, Christians should also fast from such common things

as the telephone, the television, and the theater. In each case, denying a desire or need helps us to focus better on God as the true solution to our ultimate desires and needs. As Christians fast, the self-discipline and demand for patience lead them to reflect upon their deeper need to depend on God and patiently trust in His timing.

Thus one benefit that is derived from encouraging couples to remain celibate before marriage is the patience and self-control it teaches them. Then when two people finally marry, they both can know full well that they are marrying someone who has the ability to delay gratification and control his/her urges. They can be assured that their marriage is founded on patience and a proper foundation. They are not marrying because they are quickly losing control. Unfortunately, the singles' sex triangle does not promote this type of patience and self-control—it encourages the very opposite.

Celibacy, even during engagement, is much like a fast before a big meal. It makes the person appreciate the meal more and savor the tastes. I remember a time when I fasted from food for several days to pray intensely for the health of a family member. I wanted to break the fast with a meal that would be easy to digest, so I fixed a pasta salad. Never have I enjoyed a simple meal so much, and never has pasta salad tasted so wonderful. Though this was not the primary reason for my fast, it certainly turned out to be a welcome benefit.

In the singles' sex triangle model, couples are urged to experience more and more, keeping only that final act of penetration for the wedding night. This would be parallel to recommending that someone just fast from the main course but be allowed to fill up on all the appetizers available. The person's eventual enjoyment of the main course would be spoiled. A person who fasts only from the main course is just fooling himself or herself; that would not be a fast in its true intent. It is an excuse for indulgence, not an experience of dependence. It is a detour, not a discipline. Couples whose only goal is to remain virgins in the technical sense (avoiding penetration) are also indulging themselves. Such a virginity is not virginity in its true intent. It is just an excuse, a rationalization.

PROBLEMS WITH THE TRIANGLE: CLARITY

The comparison of temporary sexual celibacy with temporary fasting from food is helpful in pointing out yet another problem with the singles' sex triangle ethic. By denying oneself in the physical arena, a person's other senses and insight tend to become more sensitive. For instance, during the extended fast that I mentioned earlier, I was praying not for myself but for a family member. And yet the longer I prayed and went without food, it seemed the real issue became not the illness in someone else but some blind spots in my own life. Towards the end, I was overcome with a strong conviction that I had to make some apologies to people I had offended, and I had to make them before I ended the fast.

So with much fear and trembling, I called up a few people and asked if I could drop by their homes. Once inside, I explained what I was feeling, accepted responsibility for the way I had caused them pain, and asked for forgiveness. What a healing experience (at least for me)! Driving home for the fast-breaking meal, I felt as if a ton of bricks had been lifted off my shoulders. It was such a powerful experience that I almost forgot the primary reason for my fast. One of the greatest benefits of fasting from food is that it helps one see issues more completely and clearly.

The same is true with the physical fasting that is usually called premarital celibacy. When a couple who desires to be intimate physically chooses to abstain, it will heighten their insight and awareness into other areas of their relationship. Conversely, if couples become too involved sexually, that can actually inhibit true love from developing.

This is especially true in terms of communication. Sexual involvement may keep two people from really getting to know one another. Couples that get too deeply involved physically often find that to be the consuming part of their relationship—to the deprivation of all other aspects. They don't talk together as much, they don't read the Bible as often, and they don't pray with as much intensity or introspection.

A discussion between Walter Trobisch and one of his counselees, Miriam, clearly illustrates this. Miriam and Timothy were engaged to be married. Trobisch began the discussion in a straightforward manner. "What worries me the most about your relationship is the fact that you are evidently not able to talk together. Timothy didn't even know how old you were, Miriam, nor how much education you have had, nor how much you earn. Actually, I knew more about you than Timothy did. How do you explain that?"

Miriam answered Trobisch, explaining that they had become sexually active only four weeks into their engagement.

"What does this have to do with your inability to talk together?" Trobisch asked.

"Very much," Miriam replied. "It soon became the main thing, the main reason for our dates. We knew that when we met we would end up uniting. We thought just of this one thing. Everything else became secondary."[4]

Timothy and Miriam's case is tragically common. Couples often know each other physically before marriage but don't discover who the other person really is until after the wedding. That's one reason that married life can be such a rude awakening for so many people. They don't know the person they married, except in a sexual way. That's one reason why as a pastor I ask couples who are sleeping together to abstain until the marriage. I try to explain the positive side of single sexuality—that temporary celibacy is a way of asserting and protecting value. Usually they are quite enthusiastic about working on giving their future marriage a solid moral foundation.

When a couple truly fast from sexual involvement, their lives usually are affected in one of three ways. First, they may discover a whole new depth and joy in their love together. As one man said, "This temporary celibacy has taught me that even without sex I'm a lucky man to have her. In fact, I'd marry her now even if we couldn't have sex!" Second, they may realize that their relationship was fairly vacuous without sex. As a result, they begin to work on improving the other areas of intimacy, the social, intellectual, emotional, and spiritual areas. Some seek out Christian counselors to help them with problem areas, such as family history, step-parent issues, or dealing with the exspouse. In this way, they end up with a much stronger and more balanced marriage than they ever would have had without premarital abstinence.

The third way couples are affected is that they may reconsider their engagement. Some couples discover that sex was the magnet that held them together, and that without it they have no relationship. Many couples decide at that point to call off the wedding.

I remember a couple where the woman, Alice, deeply wanted to agree to temporary abstinence before their marriage, while her fiancé, Terry, was extremely angry at me for even suggesting it. They had made an appointment with me because they wanted a quick wedding, and they thought I would casually agree to perform their marriage quickly. They were shocked when I refused to marry them on their timetable and under the present conditions. I clearly stipulated that I would not marry them unless they agreed to remain celibate until the marriage. Terry was furious and told Alice that they should just find another minister to marry them. But something motivated Alice to go along with my suggestions. Terry tried to talk her out of it, but Alice held to her decision. As a result, Terry was without sex for a while.

During that time, he began to notice some things about her that had escaped his attention before. In fact, he made a startling discovery— he decided that Alice was emotionally unstable and quite manipulative.

The hardest lesson for him to admit was that this was especially true sexually—she had used sex to control him. The very thing that Terry liked so much was the tool she was using to trick and capture him.

Terry broke up with Alice, and both of them felt quite devastated. But God wasn't finished in their lives. His grace and kindness always exceeds even our wildest dreams. In time Terry met another beautiful Christian woman and developed a much healthier relationship. Alice too met a new man, but this new guy was very different from Terry. Like Alice, he was an emotional and sensitive person, so was much better suited for her. He even viewed as assets what Terry had seen as liabilities. They too were able to develop a healthy, Christian relationship. Both new couples eventually wed and to this day have strong, healthy, Christian marriages.

I don't see Alice much anymore; she and her new husband moved away because of a job transfer. But Terry and his new wife are still actively involved in our church, and I have the unique pleasure of witnessing the joy they bring each other and others. I have never brought up the subject of Alice to Terry, and I thought it would become a part of the forgotten past. But one day Terry and I were in a group of couples when man named Bob related the story about "a horrible minister" who refused to marry him and his new wife.

"What kind of holier-than-thou jerk," this man complained, "would refuse to marry someone. I mean, who I marry is my business, not his. Marrying is his job—I should've sued him for discrimination and emotional damages."

As the only minister in the circle, I was feeling pretty uncomfortable with this diatribe. I was deep in thought, trying to figure out a caring and yet assertive response, when Terry beat me to the punch.

He said, "I know just what you mean. I was engaged to get married once, and a minister refused to marry us. Was I ever mad. I would lie awake at night just thinking of ways that I could get even with that guy. But then some other things happened, and I learned that the woman I was engaged to was really messed up. I just couldn't see it because I was so hot and heavy to get married. What a fool I was. I almost made the biggest mistake of my life. So I broke up with her, and pretty soon met my wife, Julie. Now I thank God for that guy who had the guts to say no to me when I needed it most."

Bob huffed and puffed a bit and then changed the subject. When the group later dispersed, Terry walked away with me. When it was just the two of us, he leaned over and quietly said, "Hey Rick, I meant what I said. I never have thanked you for what you did 'cause I was just too embarrassed to bring it up. But I think about it all the time. I almost totally messed up my life. I was mad at you for a while, but I hope you'll forgive me for it. I really appreciate now that you told me no when I needed to hear it most. Thanks."

"You're welcome, Terry," I said. "That's what friends are for."

Because of that experience, the depth of our friendship was greater than ever before. As close friends know, the strength of quality friendships is forged on the anvil of tough love. There is no other way.

PROBLEMS WITH THE TRIANGLE: BROKEN ENGAGEMENTS

The singles' sex triangle has one other problem I must point out, even though engaged couples hate to hear this. Engagement is not marriage, and couples sometimes "fall out" of engagement. Whenever I bring this point up to an engaged pair, one or both will say, "Well, that may happen to some couples. But it won't happen to us!" Of course, all of us tend to view ourselves as the exception. "Other couples may struggle, but we won't."

That's similar to married couples who struggle. Trouble often appears, and divorce is a fact of life. However, when husbands and wives are told to nurture their marriages, they sometimes say, "Others may have trouble in their marriage, but not us. Others may get a divorce, but that will never happen to us." How much better to admit that it might be a possibility and prevent it by preparing for struggles in advance. A married couple that realizes money can be a source of conflict will be much better equipped to deal with financial issues than a couple that naively assumes it won't be a problem for them.

In the same way, an engaged couple should admit to themselves that sometimes engagements are broken, and it could happen to them. If the couple proceeds merrily after the model of the singles' sex triangle and becomes heavily involved physically, they will discover the breakup even harder to bear. Because of this possibility, wise couples will keep their sexual involvement to a minimum.

Juan and Monique were deeply committed Christians who learned this truth. Juan had grown up in the church and was a gifted singer and a lay leader in the church choir. Monique moved to the city from another state, and since she too loved to sing, she joined the choir. There they met and immediately were attracted to one another.

As musicians, they both were romantics, so their dating life began in storybook fashion full of roses, candlelight dinners, and music. Soon they were deeply in love and were talking marriage. After dating only a couple of months, they became engaged.

Along with the engagement, they felt permitted to become more involved sexually, though they both wanted to reserve "the act," as they called it, until marriage. And though they did everything but the act, they were able to control that final desire. Yet as their passion and intimacy escalated, other things were disintegrating. There were things about Juan that bothered Monique, and vice versa. And as is common with couples that drew together quickly, their relationship fell apart quickly. Before they realized it, the engagement was off and there was an impenetrable wall between them. They were still able to be cordial with one another in church, but without respect.

As Monique said, "Whenever I see Juan I can't help but think about the things we did together sexually. I don't respect myself, and I certainly don't respect him. Because it was tough to see him and because I felt unworthy, I quit the choir. But I think now I may even have to find another church to attend. I can't worship with him up in front, still singing in the choir.

"I know this sounds terrible, but I can't help it—I see him up there and imagine him without any clothes on. It sort of spoils my ability to worship! In fact, it has messed up my whole walk with God. I wonder if I ever will be able to forgive myself and get these images out of my mind.

"I wonder sometimes what would happen if I told everyone about the things we did together. Would they let him stand up front still? Would they kick us both out of the church? What a fool I was. I wish I could go back in time and do things differently. But I was so sure that we were going to be married and that that would make everything OK. Was I ever wrong."

The best course of action, Monique realized in hindsight, was to keep sexual involvement to a minimum—even during engagement. As a result, in our church I often ask engaged couples two questions to help them think through this issue: (1) If you were to break up, would you still be able to be friends? Don't get involved so deeply sexually that if you broke the engagement, it would be an embarrassment to see each other socially. (2) Married couples have sex and everyone knows it. It's socially acceptable. They don't worry about their family and friends discovering what they do together in private. How about you? Do you worry about being discovered? Would you be comfortable telling your family and friends about what you do together in private?

These may seem extreme questions, but for the many couples who date and do not marry, they are crucial. The truth of the matter is that a person will usually date several people before finding his or her eventual marriage partner. Many people will even be engaged a few times before actually making it all the way through a marriage ceremony. To put it bluntly, no one is married until he or she is married. And even if a couple begins dating, becomes sexually involved, and still marry, that doesn't mean that they will not carry some baggage or guilt into their life together. And it doesn't imply that such a couple would recommend to others that it's OK to be sexually involved before marriage.

Tonya eventually became engaged to her boyfriend after six and one half years of dating, but she lost her virginity during her first year and remained sexually active up to their engagement. They are planning to occupy a four-bedroom home they recently purchased and look forward to starting a family once married. But she recommends against about extended sexual intimacy before marriage, calling it Russian Roulette.

> My story is a happy one, yet I know of too many who do not turn out like this, which is why I say that my circumstances are ones of pure luck since I never got a disease, never got pregnant, and stayed with him. Even though my story is good, I would still say people should wait for marriage for sex because it's like Russian Roulette; you never know whether it's your lucky day or not.

Questions for Discussion
1. What advantages are there to short engagements? What advantages are there to long ones?
2. Are you a patient person? Why or why not?
3. What do you think about the spiritual discipline of fasting? Do you fast? Why or why not? How is fasting helpful to spiritual growth?
4. Have you ever known a couple who could not see their own relationship objectively ? Why do you think they lacked clarity? What could they do to get a better picture of themselves?
5. Some engagements are broken. Have you ever experienced a broken engagement? How did it affect you? What did its failure teach you about love? What did it teach you about sexuality?

CHAPTER ELEVEN

HOW FULL IS YOUR MORAL BANK ACCOUNT?

The singles' sex triangle is rife with problems and pitfalls. Rather than helping singles develop patience, it makes them impatient. Rather than teaching self-control, it encourages self-indulgence. And rather than helping singles grow spiritually, it tends to create intense spiritual dissonance. It creates more problems than it solves. It asks more questions than it answers. But most tragically, it leaves singles and couples feeling bankrupt rather than valuable.

As I struggled to deal with the problems inherent in the singles' sex triangle, I came to realize that one ingredient is missing from the model. Not surprisingly, it is the same thing that is also missing from our contemporary culture's view of single celibacy—value. The downfall of the singles' sex triangle is that it doesn't help couples build a moral sense of self-worth and value. Instead, the sex triangle ignores the central theme of our value as singles: celibacy is a way of protecting and asserting value.

A NEW GUIDE TO SINGLE SEXUALITY

So I made a simple change to the singles' sex triangle and came up with a much better model, which can guide singles in their sexual behavior. I call it the Singles' Value Triangle. This triangle adds value to one side.

The Singles' Value Triangle

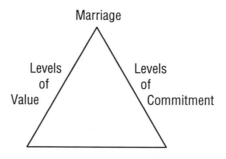

Marriage

Levels of Value

Levels of Commitment

This new triangle replaces the side representing levels of physical intimacy with levels of value. *Levels of value* means the mutual sense of value and esteem that each person in the relationship feels. As a couple begin to date and their level of commitment slowly rises, my suggestion is that this should be matched by a corresponding rise in their mutual feelings of physical and personal self-worth.

In chapters 9 and 10 we have seen how the singles' sex triangle does not protect mutual value for the couple. In chapter 11 we now consider how the singles' value triangle can guard our sexual value.

The value triangle reminds us that our sexuality is like an expensive and fragile gift. God has wrapped and boxed our sexuality carefully, and we must unwrap this gift just as carefully to fully appreciate its value and inner beauty. As we consider this new model of sexual ethics for single adults, we will learn to unwrap this gift carefully.

THE VALUE TRIANGLE AND FINANCES

Looking at the singles' sex triangle, it is easy to understand what is meant by the two sides; but in the singles' value triangle, the value side is admittedly more difficult to grasp. Can self-worth or a sense of mutual value be quantified or measured? And how can such a triangle guide sexual conduct? Though these questions seem tough at first, they actually are not all that difficult for singles, because most singles already live out a value triangle in the area of finances. In fact, the way that couples relate financially can also be illustrated with our value triangle diagram. The singles' finance triangle looks like this:

The Singles' Finance Triangle

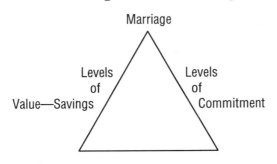

The singles' finance triangle suggests that the higher the level of mutual commitment, the more a couple should save their funds in order to begin their marriage upon a solid financial foundation. This transforms their relationship. As they increasingly value the other person, this affects one area most singles value highly, their finances. As a result, how they treat their budgets and spending will change. Though couples may spend lavishly in the early dating period, they usually cut back on the extravagances and begin to save, as they begin to talk about marriage. It is the rare couple that does not realize the importance of building a solid financial foundation before marriage.

Sometimes this transformation can be shocking to family and friends. For me, this has never been truer than when it happened in my own family. My older brother was a sort of wild guy who loved three things in life—hunting, fast cars, and riding his Harley-Davidson motorcycle. Randy called me one evening with the great news that he was getting married soon and asked if I would be his best man. I was honored and said yes, but I also expressed some skepticism. I hadn't even known that he was dating anyone. So I said, "Sure, Randy. I'd love to be your best man. Let me take you out to dinner, and we can talk about it." My plan was to get him by himself and try to talk some sense into him—to at least get him to postpone the date a bit. I thought that if we could spend some time alone together, I could get him to admit that he was rushing into this thing and wasn't really ready to marry.

So we went out to dinner and had a great time. I took him to his favorite restaurant, which served his favorite dinner—barbequed beef ribs. I can still remember trying to talk between bites of ribs, hands messy from the sauce and teeth straining to pull the meat from the bones. Between bites and wipes and trips to the salad bar, he told me all about his fiancée, how he had met her, and about their decision to marry. He also was frank about the rough spots in their romance and about how they still had plenty of areas to grow in. Then he noted that neither of them had much money, so they were trying to save as much as possible.

I thought the time had come for my big push. I said, "Randy, it sounds to me like you two have something really great going but aren't quite ready to get married. Why don't you just give yourself a few more months before the wedding?"

He was visibly hurt by my suggestion and said in an angry voice, "Forget it. She's the right woman for me, and this is the right time. We are ready!"

"Prove it to me," I said. "Just give me one solid piece of proof that will show me that you are really ready, and then I will believe you and totally support you. Think about it for a minute, and then give me your best answer."

He even stopped eating the ribs to give my question some serious thought. Finally, his eyes lit up with an answer that he knew would satisfy me. "Rick," he said, "I sold my Harley!"

"You what?" I said, shocked beyond belief.

"Yeah—I sold my Harley a week ago. I'm using the money to pay off some bills. So you still think I'm not ready?"

"No, Randy. You've convinced me. And I'm behind you 100 percent!"

My brother's decision to sell his most valued possession showed the depth of his love and commitment for his fiancée. He loved her enough to sacrifice for her, and, as the commitments became greater, so too became his willingness to sacrifice. He was making his way up the singles' finance triangle very nicely.

Finances are just one parameter of the value side of the triangle. Our money and possessions, after all, are among those things important to us, those things we value. What happened to Randy and his fiancée happens to almost every couple that decides to move up the scale of commitments. They realize that in order to support their commitments, they will have to get their financial houses in order and sacrifice in order to save the necessary money.

I know one man who decided to stop eating out every day for lunch and began brown-bagging it. Another man sold his toys—his boat and jet skis—to reduce his monthly debt load. One woman joined a car pool rather than make the hour commute alone, while another gave up her private apartment and rented a room in order to save a bit more each month. A man who was marrying a woman with two young children sold his pride and joy—an expensive sports car—and bought a used minivan.

There are no hard and fast rules on this triangle, but each person is required to be responsible. Each has to realize that any purchase he/she makes now will make their financial future more difficult. If one of them asked a financial counselor, "Well, how much can I spend? Can I buy a $100 coat or a $200 CD player?" the best answer is *not* to set an arbitrary limit. Instead the couple should redirect their focus from how much they can spend to how much they can save.

This simple economic triangle is parallel to the singles' value triangle, and the comparison can provide guidance. Just as committed couples sacrifice and save financially in order to give their new marriage a solid financial foundation, committed couples also sacrifice and save themselves sexually in order to build together a solid moral foundation for their future. As a couple sacrifices and saves themselves sexually, they slowly build considerable value in their moral bank account. On the other hand, if they spend all they have sexually, they will be bankrupt morally and have nothing to found their future upon.

Clearly, the levels of value on the singles' value triangle can be measured in terms of physical intimacy, but physical intimacy is neither the sole nor primary element to valuing the other person. We will consider specific physical parameters shortly. For now, let's consider some guideline questions to help us determine how our actions can communicate value to the other person: "Do the things I say to him communicate that I think he is a valuable person?" "Do the places I take her communicate that I value her?"

Careful attention to these questions can guide singles in concrete ways. For instance, if a woman is concerned that her male friend feel valued by her, she will avoid sarcastic humor, no matter how funny it may seem at the moment. In the same way, a man will avoid all cutting remarks, since such comments make a person feel cheap rather than valuable. Neither Joan Rivers nor Don Rickles are good role models for the couple that wants to advance up the singles' value triangle. In this simple manner, a couple can actually find specific guidance from the singles' value triangle: anything that makes another person feel devalued is not allowed; anything that builds up the other person is encouraged.

How does this all apply to sex? The guiding paradigm throughout this book has been that sex is intended for *value* and that positive celibacy is God's method of helping singles to protect and assert their own self-worth. How we allow our own bodies to be treated either builds up or tears down our own feelings of self-worth, and how we treat other people either contributes to or subtracts from their sense of personal value. The question that singles can focus upon is not, "What can't we do together sexually?" but instead is, "How much value do we want to base our relationship upon?" And since we have learned that celibacy is a way of asserting and protecting value, it follows that the best way to build a foundation of mutual value is for a couple to practice positive celibacy.

THE SINGLES' SEX TRIANGLE REVISITED

How will this affect the sexual area of a relationship? Its implications are best seen in contrast with the singles' sex triangle that taught that a couple's physical relationship was to progress in a way that is equal to their commitment level. In other words, if they have no commitment, they should not be physically involved. But as soon as they start dating, they can start kissing. When they start seriously dating, they can move up to serious kissing, and when they start exclusively dating, they may have longer kisses. When they finally become engaged, they can start mega-kissing. (Though it may sound odd to classify kisses, it is an old tradition. Even the Romans divided kisses into three levels and had a word for each: *oscula* were friendly kisses, *basia* were kisses of love, and *suavia* kisses of passion.) Such a triangle would look like this:

The Singles' Sex Triangle

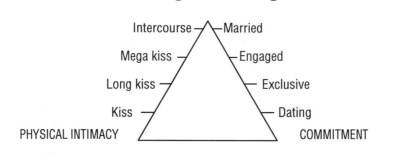

A BETTER MODEL:
THE SINGLES' VALUE TRIANGLE

But the singles' value triangle is a wholly different model, because as the levels of commitment and value rise, the physical intimacy should actually taper off. The further a couple grows in their commitment, the more they should be saving up in the terms of physical, emotional, and spiritual value. The greater their sense of commitment, the more they will feel a mutual sense of value. What would that mean in terms of physical involvement? Let's consider a couple who start holding hands and then kiss after a date or two.

As the couple become exclusive, they may begin long-kissing or even mega-kissing. But as they sense a need to develop a deeper sense of mutual respect and value in their relationship, they may decide to stop the mega-kissing. A few weeks before the wedding, they may choose to stop the long-kissing. And then just before the marriage, the couple might even decide to spend less time together and not even kiss.

Finally, they might agree to not even see each other on the morning of the wedding. Thus the old idea of not seeing the bride or groom before the wedding comes back in a more positive way. It's not a bad idea. It reflects the concept of taking some space and backing off physically right before marriage. I think such a tradition, if preceded by a gradual diminishing of physical involvement, makes perfect sense. This best of all triangles would look like this:

The Singles' Value Triangle

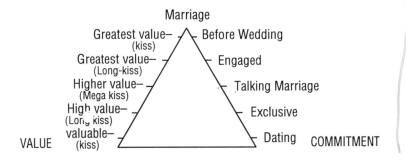

I suggest to engaged couples to look at the triangle this way and talk about what would make them feel more valuable and how their physical involvement should actually decrease the closer they approach marriage.

With this new model we can leave behind the whole notion of "What level of intimacy should we have?" and the common concern "How far can we go?" Instead, couples that want to base their marriage upon a solid foundation of moral value and mutual self-respect will ask, "How much value do we want reflected in our relationship? How valuable do we want each other to feel?" And by temporary celibacy in the dating and engagement period, couples can contribute to that sense of value.

Therefore, the closer a man and a woman get to marriage, the more they should actually back up a bit in the area of physical intimacy. What singles need most is not a new set of rules or arbitrary cut-off lines. Instead, they need a total paradigm shift, a completely different perspective on the whole question of sexual guidelines. They need to begin to think in terms of value. Of course, the value triangle makes the most immediate sense to those who are engaged and are committed to marry each other, but it also applies to all singles, whether in relationships or not.

Again, a financial example might help to illustrate the point. When I was a young single, I was frustrated by paying rent and having no equity to show for all my payments. I decided it would be a good thing to begin to save for my own home. That way, if I married some day, I would already have a home. But even if I did not marry, I would still have my own home and a base for financial security. In the same way, if a single man or woman realizes the need for building a solid foundation of self-worth, that foundation will be an asset regardless of his or her marital state.

THE TOUGH QUESTION

"Come on, Rick. Answer the really tough question—what specific acts can singles do, and what acts can't we do?"

There are many different opinions. Some authors say singles have to stop before touching breasts. Others say that anything except penetration is OK. I refuse to be a judge and jury that hands down decisions about what singles can and can't do. Instead, I appeal once again to the guiding principle and its application in the singles' value triangle—single celibacy is a way to protect and assert personal value. Some sexual acts are obviously costly, whereas others have a minimal cost. For instance, in my opinion if a couple is involved in oral sex, they are spending lots of their moral value that should be saved for marriage. I think a couple that kisses only is spending less and will have more saved up as a foundation for marriage. Consider this analogy: A couple decides to marry and wants to buy a house. In spite of that, they are enamored with nice cars and toys, so they buy new cars, a boat, and nice clothes. They spend all their money on these toys, plus max out their credit limits. They may have fun for a while, but when the day of the wedding comes, they will find that they have nothing left with which to purchase a house. In fact, they may be so far in debt that it will be years before they get out of the hole they have dug for themselves.

Sexual profligance is just as destructive. A couple that does not limit their premarital sexual activity may have a hard time establishing a solid marriage. If the woman becomes pregnant before marriage, they have created a debt that will make it very hard for them to have a solid moral foundation for their family later. They may even have difficulty keeping their own children from making those same sexual mistakes.

TIME TO BACK UP

What about a couple who have become physically intimate and now desire to back up sexually? Is that possible? How can a couple actually do that? And how can a person who feels sexually devalued find the road back to personal and spiritual self-worth?

To regain a sense of moral value is again parallel to getting out of financial debt. First we must acknowledge our condition. There has to be an awareness of the true situation. In the Bible, this is called repentance. In economic terms, it is called the "day of reckoning." This takes place when we realize that we can't pay for all of our purchases and that we haven't the willpower or ability to fix the problem. At some point, we admit to ourselves, "I need help."

The next step is to devise a plan of how to pay off the debt. Financial counselors help with financial planning; spiritual counselors or close friends can help in the sexual area. Financially, we may have to cut up our credit cards. Then we must begin making payments on the debts until they are paid off.

A plan also needs to be outlined in the sexual arena. A couple may decide they need to back up in their physical intimacy and base their relationship on a sense of mutual esteem and value, rather than just on physical passion. They may say, "We need to get to know each other better, talk more, experience a greater diversity of situations and see how we interact in different areas. We need to discuss plans for the future more in depth. We need to get to know each other in emotional, social, and spiritual areas, rather than concentrating on the physical aspects of our relationship." They may have to set some limits—"We will kiss but not long-kiss," or, "We will kiss but not disrobe." The couple needs to talk through the limits (such as what parts of the body can be touched), and they need to agree to mutual boundaries.

It would also be beneficial for each person to find someone to be accountable to, someone spiritually mature, someone he or she can be honest with, someone who will pray for and with him or her. But, of course, it won't work if the person is not honest with the accountability partner or does not take seriously the friend's advice. If the adviser cautions the couple about being alone for too long a time, for example, the couple must take such suggestions seriously. Or they may be instructed to go to lunch in public rather than having an intimate dinner alone at night, not to have sexual conversations on the phone, to date only in group situations, and so on. It is best if both persons agree, but even if only one person determines to do this backing off, it is worth the price and can be done.

Of course, none of these suggestions will work if the couple does not work by the plan or the guidelines they have set. And an important aspect is that each person remain in prayer and in close relationship with God.

As strange as it may seem, sometimes it's better for a couple who has gone too far to back up—even to the point of postponing their marriage—to give them time to regain a sense of personal value and self-worth. This will be like a couple who realize they have spent too much and are not in a position to get married. The financial obligations are great, for example, the wisest solution is to postpone the marriage until the couple are financially sound. In the same way, a couple who have spent themselves emotionally and physically may realize it will take them a long time to recover their sense of moral purity and value.

For singles who are sexually involved, such a backing off or postponing of marriage for a bit may serve to clear their minds and help them make wiser decisions. It may serve to help them build a better foundation for all future relationships. They may discover that the person they are with is a real treasure and be motivated to explore that relationship in depth. On the other hand, they may find that that person is the wrong match for them and utilize the wisdom and courage to break up in order to avoid a terrible mistake. No matter what happens, to back off a bit and become temporarily celibate is always a positive move. It is God's way of helping singles assert and protect a healthy sense of self-worth.

COMMITMENT AND BALANCE

The value triangle instructs couples that open, public commitments are a necessary part of relational growth and balance. The different commitments that couples make together are like steps up the side of the triangle. It is at this point that a problem can occur—the couple's perception of what commitments should occur at what level may differ. So let's now consider just the commitment side of the value triangle.

During one counseling session I asked a couple, Loretta and Ed, to fill in the commitment side of the triangle—without showing the other person. Loretta's triangle was labeled like this:

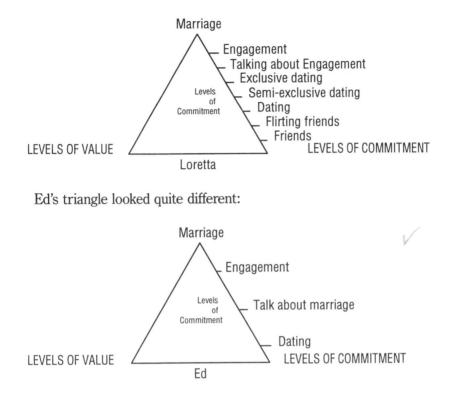

When they showed each other their completed triangles, they both were astounded. Loretta said, "Ed, this really bugs me. Here we are talking about marriage, and you are barely halfway up your triangle! And you don't even have exclusive dating on your chart. You mean you would talk about marriage with more than one woman at a time?"

Ed didn't answer. He was in a no-win situation. If he was honest and admitted it, she would be angry. If he lied, he would be dishonest. Besides, she would guess it and be mad anyway.

I recommend that couples take out pen and paper and actually do this exercise together. They each should draw triangles, fill them in separately, and then compare triangles. This can be fun if done early in the relationship, and it can be referred to again and again throughout the courtship. The triangles don't have to be fancy—I've seen them on the backs of restaurant placemats, on napkins, on computer printouts, and on scratch paper. Whatever the method, the important thing is to do this early in the relationship and discuss them completely and in honesty. If a couple has different levels of commitment (not a huge problem), they need to work through that together.

Questions for Discussion:
1. If you have ever been engaged, did you experience the singles' finance triangle? Did you both start saving? Why or why not?
2. The key to this book is that sex is intended for value—how we treat others (and allow ourselves to be treated) should communicate and protect value. In your dating past, did you feel valued sexually? Why or why not?
3. This new model suggests that couples should actually back off sexually before the marriage. How to you think that would affect the honeymoon? Why?
4. Are you a patient person? Why or why not?
5. How can a couple continue to grow together if they have gone too far sexually? Name some specific things they could do in the different areas of life: emotional, physical, social, intellectual, and spiritual.
6. Have you ever known a couple who could not see their own relationship objectively? Why do you think they lacked clarity? What could they do to get a better picture of themselves

CHAPTER TWELVE

WHAT ABOUT LIVING TOGETHER BEFORE MARRIAGE?

Should Christian couples live together before marriage? What about living together if they are engaged? How does the value approach affect the issues of living together, engagement, and commitment.

In order to deal with these questions, we now should ask, What is commitment anyway; is it the same as being exclusively with one person? What was the nature of commitment and sexuality in biblical times? Those two questions are important and will be addressed in this section. But first, let's consider a more fundamental question about our sexuality: Why can't sex be something that two people can just enjoy together without any strings attached? That sure would simplify things, some advocates of living together claim.

SEX AND COMMITMENT

First, we must remember that sex is not a mere biological desire that needs to be fulfilled as does our appetite for food (see chapters 5–6). Sex is much more than mere biology—it is God's guarantee that we will not give in to our tendency toward isolation but will instead become relational people. The sex drive keeps us working on friendships, forgiving each other, and being willing to give love one more try even after the pain of betrayal. It keeps us believing in love and investing in intimacy. Because of our sexuality, we are driven to fulfill the deepest potential within us—to reflect the very nature of God by loving and being loved.

Second, real love and intimacy is delicate and fragile. It is full of value and potential, much like a young fruit tree. If cared for properly, a fruit tree will produce a harvest for years to come. But to protect and nurture this tree, the gardener must be committed to its care, willing to spend much energy and attention to it. Otherwise it can be easily damaged, even destroyed. Planted in the wrong place, the tree may be trampled and ruined. Watered improperly, it will remain small and become stunted and sterile. Left unprotected, it can become food for some gopher or a rabbit; within minutes the little animal can strip the tree of its bark and kill it.

Little rabbits may not seem ferocious, but they can devastate a garden. For four years I lived in a small but beautiful area northwest of Los Angeles County called Conejo Valley. I quickly discovered the origin of its name: thousands of little rabbits—*conejos* in Spanish—ran wild. At first I considered them to be cute little creatures, and I enjoyed watching them hop out of the bushes or across the road. But after I planted some fruit trees in my yard, my opinion of them changed. I discovered that those cute bunnies made their living by sneaking into gardens and stripping the bark off the base of young saplings.

One night the *conejos banditos* savaged my trees. I didn't notice the damage the next day, but several days later the trees appeared to be sick. I looked closely, and the trees, though still standing, were bare from ground level to about a foot above the ground. The nursery expert told me there was nothing I could do. Trees die when their bark is stripped in a full circle around their trunks. All he could recommend was that I buy and install small plastic protectors to put around the base of the remaining trees or that I paint the trunks with a special paint that the varmints don't like.

In other words, if my trees were to grow into maturity and bear any fruit, they had to be protected. The rabbits were just one of many dangers that my trees would face; they also needed protection against insects, drought, frost, and disease. I had never realized that growing fruit trees was such a big deal.

The same principle applies to a new friendship or love; it needs to be protected from all sorts of dangers and diseases. That's why sexual expression in the Bible is always related to commitment. Commitment is the safe, fertile, protected environment that allows the "tree" of love to grow. A quality commitment is like the shields that I wrapped around the base of those young trees. With a quality commitment, the new relationship will have a chance to live and grow. Without it, the relationship will surely die.

Let's apply this now to the subject of singles and sexuality. According to the Bible, sexual and genital intimacy are appropriate when protected by the appropriate commitments. But if such commitments are lacking, sexual expression is inappropriate—in some cases so inappropriate as to incur the death penalty (in the Mosaic law). Why is this the case? Why is commitment such a big deal? And isn't being with one person in an exclusive relationship a sign of deep commitment?

COMMITMENT IN THE BIBLE

Commitment is a key concept in the Bible, though the idea often goes unnoticed because it is cloaked in religious language. In Hebrew, the primary word for commitment is *berith,* while in Greek the word is *diatheke.* In Jerome's Latin translation of the Bible, the Vulgate, both words are translated by *testamentum,* from which we derive our English word *testament.* A testament is simply a covenant, an agreement. It is similar to our modern words *commitment, contract,* and *deal.* All of these words would today be apt translations of *berith* and *diatheke.* So central was this word to biblical theology that Jerome labeled the two parts of the Bible *Vetus Testamentum* and *Novum Testamentum,* from which we get the titles Old Testament and New Testament. What this means is that the two parts of the Bible could better be translated today Old and New Covenants, Old and New Commitments, Old and New Contract, or even Old and New Deal. A covenant or testament is simply an agreement between two parties, usually qualified by two requirements: mutuality and legality. A covenant is considered valid if it is mutually entered into and agreed upon, and if it is recognized as binding by the community.

But there are exceptions to both conditions. Concerning the requirement of mutuality, for example, some covenants are one-sided; they are known as unilateral covenants. An example of this would be the parents' commitment to love a new child. The child is incapable of agreeing to an arrangement with the parents, but tho parents nonetheless bind themselves to their new offspring. They commit themselves (usually implicitly, but it can also be made explicit) to loving their new child regardless of response. The parents will love unilaterally, even in the face of open rebellion (a common occurrence in the teenage years). God's commitment to love Israel is also an example of a unilateral commitment. God's love toward Israel is still active, even though they have rejected Jesus, God's own Son and their Messiah (see Romans 11).

In spite of such exceptions, most commitments still carried the two requirements of mutuality and legality. This was especially true in the area of sexuality. If a man wanted to lie with a woman but did so without her consent and without the approval of the community, he was judged as having committed the terrible crime of rape. For instance, when Shechem raped Dinah, the daughter of Jacob and Leah, Dinah's brothers were unwilling to forgive Shechem—even though Shechem wanted to marry Dinah and pay whatever bridal price her family designated (Genesis 34). They refused Shechem's offer of marriage and the generous bridal price, and instead killed every male relative of Shechem. In their minds, the crime of rape could not just be swept under the carpet but demanded vengeance. Shechem's crime was so heinous because he tried to divorce sexuality from commitment and disregarded both of the requirements of mutuality and legality.

But what if it had not been a rape; what if Dinah were a willing partner and yet betrothed to another man? His case would have been little improved, because it would have still lacked the requirement of legality. This requirement, codified in the Mosaic Law, made both people guilty and subject to death (Deuteronomy 22:23).

If the virgin girl was not betrothed to another man and willingly has sexual union with the man, the situation was only slightly different: Instead of the death penalty, a bridal price had to be paid. "If a man seduces a virgin who is not pledged to be married and sleeps with her, he must pay the bride-price, and she shall be his wife. If her father absolutely refuses to give her to him, he must still pay the bride-price for virgins" (Exodus 22:16–17). Thus, even mutual consent by the individuals was not enough to make a couple married.

A COMMON MISUNDERSTANDING

This flies in the face of a common misunderstanding of marriage in the Old Testament. This common misunderstanding is that in the Old Testament, marriage occurred whenever two people expressed personal commitments to one another, not during a later public ceremony or recognition. Therefore, it was acceptable for the couple to be involved sexually after betrothal and before the marriage ceremony or feast. An example of this thinking is Bishop John Shelby Sprong's brave but misguided work, *Living in Sin?—A Bishop Rethinks Human Sexuality.* Sprong writes,

> I call on churches of this land to revive a concept of betrothal and to install it as a valid option and a sign of a serious commitment, even though it falls short of the legal status of marriage. In many ancient societies a man and a woman were pledged long before they were married. That betrothal sometimes meant that they

were bound in a relationship of commitment that, in some instances, permitted sexual activity. That institution of betrothal met very real social and economic needs in those ancient societies. There are today quite different social and economic needs in our society, which perhaps a newly defined and revived institution of betrothal would meet once again.

I am proposing that we revive the word, with a new definition. By "betrothal" I mean a relationship that is faithful, committed, and public, but not legal or necessarily for a lifetime. . . . To make it a bit broader I would include the somewhat more vague category of "an engagement to be engaged."[1]

As Sprong himself notes, this idea of allowing sexual expression in an engaged or pre-engaged state is not new. Unfortunately, this raises more problems and questions than it answers: If the commitment is not for a lifetime, then precisely what length of time is it for? Ten years? Ten months? Ten days? And how would a pregnancy be handled? He claims, "The conception and birth of children would not be appropriate to this relationship of betrothal"[2]. But what about the couples who, even though they take precautions, find themselves pregnant? And what of the couples that choose to dissolve the semicommitment?

The relationship of commitment to physically intimacy was discussed in detail in chapter 9. But many still accept Sprong's faulty interpretation; consider, for instance, the two case studies in "A Single Speaks." Both believed the lie that sex before marriage is acceptable to God. Both have regretted their decisions.

A SINGLE SPEAKS

One Woman's Story

In my high school youth group, I was told by our youth minister that fornication and adultery were sins that could be committed only after marriage. That's what I wanted to hear, and I became sexually involved with the man I hoped to marry—but didn't! I do feel that if I had known what fornication meant then, I would have understood that sex before marriage was wrong even if it was with the one you were planning on marrying. I would not have gotten involved in it, since at that time in my life I was very conscientious about obeying God. But since I saw adultery as something committed only after marriage and didn't know that fornication meant sex outside of marriage, I was under the impression that this was an area that God didn't address.

Then a friend told me that he learned in college that having sex, in the Old Testament, was the same thing as getting married. Because of all these things, I weakened my defenses and gave in. It was only years later through much pain and searching that I came to a more enlightened view. I really feel a disservice was done to me by my youth pastor and church in this area.

One Man's Story

I started dating my [future] wife as soon as I joined the church group. She was also a new Christian, but already she was so different from the other women I had dated and slept with. We were taught that a Christian couple shouldn't have intercourse before marriage, and we made that our goal. But then someone else told us that, in the Bible, engagement was the same thing as marriage; so once we were engaged, we became very active sexually. That was a really hard time for us, because we thought it was OK, but we were ashamed of it and wouldn't tell a soul about it! We even lied to the minister who married us, when he asked us in premarital counseling if we were sexually active.

In spite of what we had been told, we still knew deep inside that it was wrong. Since our marriage, we have spoken many times about how we wish we had waited, and about how we wish that "friend" hadn't been so "helpful." What naive, baby Christians we were.

The debate, however, continues, even in evangelical seminaries. Once I was part of a panel discussion entitled "Singles and Sexuality," held at a southern California seminary. The other three panel members had quite different agendas from my own. One single woman argued for the appropriateness of "full genital expression" between singles of either sex or even between singles of the same sex. The other panelists believed that all sexual expression before marriage except penetration was acceptable. I was trying to point out that temporary celibacy is a way to protect and assert value.

During an interesting and sometimes heated discussion, we all agreed on one point: sexual expression should be tied to commitment. Once we began to discuss specifically what was involved in a commitment, though, it became obvious that we again were poles apart in our views. The other panelists felt that private mutual commitment was enough to permit very intimate sexual relations. I stressed that mutual commitment was a necessary but not sufficient prerequisite. In addition to mutual, private commitment, there needed to be a public affirmation or ratification of that private commitment before any sexual expression was appropriate. This is because the success of the marriage depended not only upon private commitment, but also upon the community's commitment to honor and support the union.

This very important point is often overlooked. The union of a man and a woman, especially in biblical times, did not involve only those two people. It had great impact upon their families and communities, and its success depended on the community's recognition of that union. Sex and commitment alone did not constitute a marriage. It was commitment and the community's affirmation that created a marriage.

Many singles however, accept the idea that engagement is close to marriage in God's eyes. One man told me why his fiancée and he were sexually active. "In the Old Testament, the couple just promised to love each other and then moved in together. They didn't have any ceremony or piece of paper like today. The commitment was the marriage. We know that we are committed to each other, so we feel that in God's eyes we are married. The marriage ceremony will only make that public and legal."

"Well," I responded, "you are close to the truth. In the Old Testament, there was no piece of paper signifying marriage, only one for divorce. And even in the early church, there were no wedding ceremonies that we know of; that all came centuries later. But there is one problem with your thinking—you two are having sex in secret, whereas the couples in the Old Testament did not. Before the two of them ever went into their tent together for the first time, their families and community knew what was happening. But your family and church doesn't know what's going on. As a matter of fact, you're trying to keep it a secret.

"And even if an unmarried man and woman wanted to marry and mutually consented to sex, they were not considered married in the Bible. They would be married only after the father of the bride agreed to the union and the bridal price was paid. The marriage was not a given—the father could refuse the couple and no marriage would take place.

"So you see, you're only halfway there. The mutual commitment you share together is a great start, but you still need your community's affirmation and support. Then you will truly be married."

Like it or not, marriage is not only a personal event; it also is a cultural and community phenomenon. As long as we humans are involved in communities, the success of any commitment is dependent on the respect the community gives to that commitment. A tragically common and extreme example would be the rape of a married woman. In that violent instance, the marriage commitment between her and her husband is not respected by the other community member that perpetrated the crime, and the negative consequences are crippling. Many marriages have been destroyed because they could not endure the scars that result from rape.

A less extreme example can be seen in a woman who becomes attracted to her married male co-worker. If she respects his marriage commitment, she will not act out her attraction and nothing will ever come of it. But if she does not respect his commitment, she may flirt, make suggestive comments, and actually proposition him. If his marriage is struggling (as every marriage does at some point), her aggressiveness may have destructive consequences.

Let me give a lighter example. Sometimes singles begin to date, but they try to keep their romance secret from their other single friends or from the church singles group. They do this for many reasons: some are very private people, others want to keep their options open, still others are afraid of failure. But whatever the motivation for secrecy, the community is unable to respect their commitment and can actually make it tougher on them. Other guys may keep asking the woman out on dates, not knowing that she is seeing one man exclusively. Other women may show similar attention to the man, inviting him to dinner or to the theater. This couple has much more pressure on them because of their decision to be secretive. They have to deal not only with each other, but also with all the other interested parties. How much easier it would be for the couple to be open and honest with their friends about their budding romance. The friends can treat their beginning steps up the ladder of commitment with respect and understanding. They can offer encouragement, advice, and keep their distance. In addition, friends can pray for God's blessing on the new couple. But all these benefits are forfeited if the budding commitment is not made public.

Among baby boomers and post-boomers, the "C" word is not always well received. Commitment means time, energy, and of course, the possibility of rejection. Some won't move toward increasing levels of commitment for fear of pain, the pain of losing the person they care for. But if we value someone, and our care for the person deepens, we must continue the journey to deeper commitment. When we do that, we give room for love to blossom and a fuller intimacy to occur. We can know the other person better; we can help him or her more; and we surely learn to value the person more deeply.

THE REAL TEST

Remember that both sides of the singles' value triangle work together. Increasing commitment means granting the other person greater value. How will this affect a deep commitment—say, engagement? When singles start dating, enter into exclusive relationships, and the fires of passion are enflamed, it gets tough to abstain, even if that is what the couple wants to do. Some singles try to withstand the temptations by the strength of their personal willpower. Still others know they can't do it and ask God for supernatural willpower. But in spite of prayers, discussions, and resolutions, sexual desire does not diminish in Christian relationships as dating proceeds. Once the relationships begin, there is an enormous pull toward sexual activity.

At some time in a romantic relationship, particularly during engagement, the desire for physical intimacy and for sexual activity can grow in strength, and the expression of physical love probably will seem a very natural response. As a pastor I have found that the "wait until marriage" theology of single sexuality loses its influence for engaged couples as the marriage approaches. It works somewhat for those who have no love interest, but for those who feel that God has blessed them with a future marriage partner, it becomes more difficult to wait as the wedding date approaches.

Repeatedly I have heard engaged Christian couples, even church leaders and seasoned, dedicated Christians, confess in premarital counseling that they have become sexually active. As one professional, conservative seminary-trained, single man (let's call him Jeff and his fiancée Julie) said, "Yes, we are involved sexually." Immediately after this confession, he, like other singles, launched into a passionate defense of their sexual activity.

"You've got to understand, Rick, that we believe God has brought us together and this marriage is His will. We think that in His eyes we are already married, even though the public ceremony hasn't taken place yet. The ceremony will just confirm for everyone else what has already taken place in our hearts."

"Why have a ceremony, then?" I asked.

"Its a cultural, legal, and family thing," Jeff responded. "The spiritual event has already happened in our commitment to each other. The ceremony just affirms that commitment. It doesn't create it."

"Thon why do you want a church wedding," I asked, "if it's not a spiritual event? Why not call a justice of the peace or a judge to officiate?"

"Well, we are Christians, of course. We made our commitment before God. God is the center of our life together, so we want the ceremony to reflect that."

This short account of a much longer conversation just displays that intelligent Christians can and do rationalize and defend most anything, given enough time and interest in the issue. At this point in the conversation, I felt pretty unimportant as their pastor. I even mused to myself, in a quick daydream played out in my head, that the whole ceremony should be adjusted to fit Jeff's view:

"Dearly beloved, we are gathered here today to witness what has already happened . . .

"Who has given away this woman a few months ago to be married to this man?

"Did you take this woman to be your wife . . .

"Did you take this man to be your husband . . .

"You may kiss your bride again . . .

"I pronounce legally what has already happened physically months ago . . ."

As I counsel sexually active Christian couples who try to to justify their involvement, I discover a legion of defenses and rationalizations. Some are weak, of course, but some are pretty good. Several times I was forced to admit silently, "Hey, that is a pretty good reason. I wonder why God said no to that?" For a time, I was able to appeal only to God's command to abstain, fully aware that guilt and obedience were the only tools I could use for leverage.

My whole approach was radically transformed and improved when I began to instruct engaged Christian couples about the positive side of single sexuality. Rather than try to convince couples that they ought to obey God, I now spend quite a bit of time teaching them God's reason for creating the idea of temporary abstinence in the first place. Understanding this positive side is not easy, because it involves grasping a completely new approach to sexuality (making a paradigm shift), but the results have been fascinating.

After learning the positive side to single sexuality, Jeff said, "Hey, I like that idea. I really want Julie to feel that she is valuable to me."

Julie then made one of her few comments. Softly, she said, "Jeff, I love you and love the way you treat me sexually, but I gotta admit that I feel sort of cheap. I mean if our family and friends found out, or if I got pregnant, I would feel like scum. I know you love me, but I don't feel very lovely."

Jeff also admitted feeling guilty about sex before marriage but blamed his weakness in that area to a lack of any positive reason to wait. But after we discussed the positive aspects, Jeff quickly changed positions and with much excitement committed himself to temporary celibacy before the marriage—not because he had to but because he wanted to. He was now being obedient to God, understood why, and was happy to do so. He was able to experience the biblical truth that "His commands are not burdensome" (1 John 5:3).

What changed the command from a burden to an opportunity? The difference was that Jeff, for the first time, grasped the positive side to his own single sexuality. The positive approach is the only thing I have found that actually helps Christian singles desire to remain celibate until the marriage night.

Because of this, I suggest that every engaged couple study this approach to biblical sexuality as a part of their premarital preparation. It provides a much needed guide to engaged sexuality, but it also helps them understand and prepare for sexual intimacy after the ceremony. Commitment plus value—that is the formula for appreciating our sexuality and finding pure joy in our sexual lives.

Questions for Discussion:
1. Have you ever heard that couples in the Bible were married when they committed to one another? When? How did that influence you?
2. If couples are married when they feel committed to one another, then what is their marital status when they don't feel committed or when one partner betrays the commitment?
3. This chapter argues that commitment, though important, is not enough. A marriage also requires a public, legal affirmation. Do you agree with this? Why or why not?
4. What do you think would happen in our culture today if we outlawed the legal side of marriage and just allowed couples to "marry themselves" and "divorce themselves"? Why are laws a valuable and necessary part of civilization?
5. Some engagements are broken. Have you ever experienced a broken engagement? How did it affect you? What did its failure teach you about love? What did it teach you about sexuality?

PART FOUR

TOUGH QUESTIONS AND VALUE-FILLED ANSWERS

CHAPTER THIRTEEN

INTIMACY, GENDER, AND COMMITMENTS

The preceding chapters don't pretend to answer every question regarding single sexuality. Instead, they present a new, positive approach to single sexuality: temporary celibacy is a way singles can assert and protect a sense of personal and physical self-worth.

Now the real work begins. We must apply this new model to the various problems and issues that singles face—fantasies, lust, masturbation, sexual compatibility, single parenting, etc. The approach from the perspective of value sheds new light on some old problems and issues. The following questions were asked by single adults who attended my sexuality seminars. During the final break, I would ask the singles to write down their questions anonymously (which allowed them to be totally honest and ask questions that they would never raise publicly). Thon in the final session I would try to give a value-oriented response to each question.

In many cases, the singles themselves contributed extraordinary insights. What follows is a compilation of my thoughts and their insights. Let's take a few of the simpler questions first and save the last chapter for the more difficult questions concerning fantasies, lust, and masturbation.

1. **There seems to be a confusing interchange of terms. Sometimes you talk about sexuality in a way that suggests physical intimacy, and sometimes not. Is there a differ-**

ence between sexual intimacy and sexuality? And if so, what is it?

The Bible says that in the beginning God created humans as male and female (Genesis 1:27). That means that we are all created as sexual beings. No one has been created without an inborn sexuality and genital apparatus. Everyone, whether he or she likes to admit it or not, is a sexual person, and therefore his or her sexuality pervades and influences every aspect of life. Sexuality is the omnipresent influence. It affects all relationships—between parents and children (fathers treat their sons differently than their daughters, for example), between brothers and sisters, and between friends (males will treat their male friends differently than their female friends and vice versa). Individual sexuality is always a part of relationships. Some people may try to deny that or pretend otherwise, but, no matter how hard they try, it is impossible to escape their inborn, gender-specific sexuality.

This can be proven by the fact that we each see life through the grid of our own experience, which is always an *embodied* experience. All that we know and understand about life is grasped through our bodies, not in spite of them. We cannot remove ourselves from our bodies and view the world from some objective vantage point. Furthermore, these bodies are either male or female, so our experience of life is relentlessly male or female. For instance, I, Rick, have only one body and mind out of which I view life—which is male. So I see life from a male perspective. In the same way, a woman sees life through her sexual perspective as a female. She cannot step outside of her sexuality in her perspective. That's why I think the increase in feminine studies today is a very positive movement; we are discovering that we can't analyze life, culture, or science, and so on, from only a male perspective.

We all wear colored glasses, and the glasses are in one of only two colors—male and female. Men see the world through their uniquely colored lenses, whereas women see the same world through differently tinted lenses. Thus the world looks different to each sex.

2. If males and females are so different, how can they come to an understanding of each other's perspective?

We can learn to appreciate what a person of the opposite sex experiences through discussion, communication, and the like, but that takes a lot of effort. The attempt to understand someone who is different from ourselves requires much work and planning. Men and women have to continually work hard at their relationships, because there is no way we can understand a person of the opposite sex without listening attentively.

Of course, even then we will never completely understand another person. There is no way we can feel or think exactly what another person feels or thinks. That's why counselors are taught to never say, "I understand what you are saying." A counselor hasn't lived through what the other person has. So instead of "I understand what you are saying," counselors are taught to reflect what they have heard and say, "Let me see if I have heard you correctly. What you are saying is . . . " Even though our experiences may be similar, our perspectives will be different because we are distinct individuals. Because of this, our experiences will *never* be exactly congruent. Of course, we should try to understand each other better. Yet as we pursue understanding the opposite sex, we must realize we cannot fully reach this goal. Our pursuit is not a curse, though. It is a blessing in disguise, because the pursuit brings excitement and adventure into relationships. A husband and wife can know each other for sixty years, and yet be surprised by each other every day. Seen in this way, sexuality is one of the lenses that most greatly affects our world view, and our sexual differences enhance the growth and development of intimacy.

3. Is intimacy, then, the process of getting to know each other better? How does this differ from sexual intimacy?

Intimacy is the gradual growth in understanding of another person by listening, discussing, sharing, being mutually involved. Intimacy can occur in many areas: emotional, social, spiritual, and the physical. Thus you can become intimate with a person and not have physical contact. But even though there is no physical contact, sexuality is involved. In this way, every relationship is a sexual relationship.

And yet, although every relationship has sexual aspects to it, I still think it is a good idea to reserve the term *sexual intimacy* primarily for physical, genital contact. However, though the term will be helpful in most cases, there are exceptions to this definition. Sometimes people can be sexually active without being sexually intimate. Conversely, two people can be sexually intimate without ever disrobing or touching genitals. An example of this would be kissing. Kissing is an area of sexual activity, and certain types of kissing are inappropriate in relationships that aren't exclusive. In fact, some women feel that certain types of kissing are more intimate than sexual intercourse. This illustrates our uniqueness as individuals; God did not make cookie-cutter people. Everyone views sexual intimacy in different ways.

Thus, if someone is going to be intimate with another person, he or she will need to find out what intimacy means to that person. To one man, intimacy may mean an honest discussion about finances or past failures. To a woman, it may mean a long silent stroll on the beach or a deep conversation of mutual vulnerability. To another person, intimacy may just refer to orgasm. To another, intimacy might refer to a certain way of kissing.

To make this even more confusing, two people can have sex without being sexually intimate. The sex act itself can be done in a very non-intimate way—on an animal level. This is sex without intimacy. A kiss, for instance, can be a non-intimate expression of affection. An extreme example would be rape. Rape involves genital activity, but it is not sexual intimacy. It is just the opposite. It is sexual abuse. Molestation would fall in the same category. Just because physical touching is involved, that does not mean intimacy is also taking place.

4. **Many writers distinguish between emotional intimacy and sexual (physical) intimacy. They say that emotional intimacy is just as intense and often as dangerous outside of marriage as sexual intimacy. Do you believe there are distinctions?**

I don't think you can make clear distinctions as some authors try to do. Emotions are involved in sexuality, even in cases where the emotional aspect is denied or put on hold. Emotional intimacy can be as damaging as sexual intimacy outside of marriage—because emotional intimacy between a man and woman always has a sexual aspect to it. Even though two people are not genitally involved, they may be more intimate than a husband and wife who have been genitally involved but are dysfunctional in other areas, as in their communication levels.

Once again, we are intrinsically sexual beings. Everything we think and feel is colored by our sexuality. So if a person has an intellectual intimacy with another person, there will be a sexual aspect to it. That's why there are appropriate and inappropriate things to do and say to someone of the opposite sex, even on a social level.

Remember, we cannot separate these spheres of our lives from each other. Instead they are like overlapping circles. They all interconnect and affect each other. I think damage is done when we try to completely separate these aspects and deny that sexuality influences our relationships. Intimacy is highly complex, and we do ourselves a disservice when we simplify it too superficially.

In my own life, I have concluded that it is healthy to admit that my friendships with women (even those other than my wife) have a sexual aspect to them. I have found that if I admit my inherent sexuality and respect its power, I can maintain a higher degree of purity and compassion. But when I try to deny the sexual aspect, the very act of denial is usually covering up some problem or issue I need to face. In the same way, singles should not be afraid of their sexuality or deny it, but recognize it, be aware of it, and respect it. If singles try to avoid or deny that truth, it can eventually resurface with destructive impact.

Unfortunately, many Christians pretend that they attend church as neutered people and that there is no sexual dimension to their relationships. This pretense about sexuality was demonstrated in some insufficient earlier attempts to promote the idea of gender equality. As a way of promoting equality, some pretended that we really didn't have sexual differences or inclinations. They attempted to eliminate the distinctiveness of male and female. But the truth is clear: though we are equal in God's eyes, we are distinct sexual beings.

5. God made us different sexually to force us to do the work of developing quality relationships. How does this perspective affect the issue of homosexuality?

Much attention today focuses on sexual discrimination and the difficulty of living out the homosexual lifestyle. That may be true on a broad, social level at this point in our history. But I would like to suggest, from a theological point of view, that rather than being a difficult lifestyle, homosexuality may be the easy way out. Some people may engage in homosexual relationships rather than make the effort to understand the perspective of the opposite sex. It's easier to have a relationship with someone of the same sex because it does not require as much effort.

Of course, homosexual practices violate both biological design and God's intent. Scripture clearly declares the behavior as sin, condemned in both the Old and New Testaments. (See Leviticus 18:22, 20:13; Romans 1:18–19, 24–27; and 1 Corinthians 6:9–11.) But why is Scripture so against homosexual behavior? Again, it is not just an arbitrary rule, a "don't" from God. God always has positive reasons for His instructions. At heart, homosexuality is wrong because homosexual practice does not challenge us to develop a deep, giving intimacy. Why is this the case?

A greater challenge exists in understanding and developing intimacy with a person of a totally different perspective than with someone who has a similar perspective. This is especially true sexually—it is much easier for a man to understand another man's sexual needs, desires, and physiology than it is for the same man to understand a woman's needs, desires, and physiology. A man can pretty much guess what would please a male partner because he already knows what pleases himself; and the same is true, of course, regarding lesbian sexuality.

Heterosexuals, on the other hand, are forced by their differing physiology to ask more questions, talk more, and listen better—which is actually an asset, because in the long run it makes the heterosexual relationship deeper and more intimate. Homosexuality, then, is a cop-out and a compromise. If sexual differentiation is that which drives us to question, listen, and communicate, then a lack of sexual differentiation will short-circuit this process and will result in lower levels of intimacy and self-worth.

6. Do men and women have equal sexual needs?

Sexual celibacy is a way of protecting and asserting value, and our sex drives are God's guarantee that we won't avoid relationships but will stay involved in building relationships of intimacy. In these two areas, each gender's needs are equal and congruent. The level of self-worth in both males and females is directly related to how they allow themselves to be treated physically. We can again go back to the $600 table illustration. How the table is treated is directly related to the value that is placed on the table. If people allow themselves to be treated poorly, it reflects that they don't have a sense of high value—either by themselves or others. Both men and women have the need to build a moral foundation for their lives. Both need to be able to see value within themselves. They can do that if they don't spend themselves sexually.

Because our culture still has vestiges of a strong patriarchialism, it tends to be the men who carry fewer scars in this area. The women are often put in the place of having to protect their virginity and are pressured by the men. Because the women are the ones who bear children, they also have to be more concerned about protection against pregnancy. But things are becoming more equal. Paternity suits are making pregnancy a matter of concern for men as well. The rise in sexually transmitted diseases makes the matter of protection, and concern over whom one is sleeping with, more of an issue for each person. Women are taught not to be so passive; they are more sexually aggressive today. In my experience in singles groups, I have had as many or more problems with women making sexual advances toward the men as I have had with the men making advances toward the women. It goes both ways.

It is a misconception to say that men have a greater sex drive than women. In my experience in counseling Christian married couples, there are just as many problems with the man's lack of desire for sex as with the woman's.

The cultural stereotype is that men are always wanting sex; if anyone doesn't want sex, it will be the woman. That is not always the case. Men may think about one aspect of sex (the physical act) more than women, but women may think of the romantic, the interpersonal, the love and caring aspects of sex more than men do. Those thoughts reflect a basic drive in sexuality, a drive toward relationships that both sexes share equally. Sex isn't just physical expression; that is only one part. Sex also includes a basic attraction and a desire to be in a relationship with another.

In most areas, men and women have equal sexual needs—the need to experience intimacy, to give and receive love. How those needs may actually appear or be acted out may be quite different, and they will also vary from person to person regardless of gender. Generalizations don't help much, because individuals are different. A man cannot deal with his spouse based on generalizations as statistically codified by sociologists. If he does, he may quit listening to her or stop picking up clues from her behavior or words. Generalizations are helpful when studying society as a whole and charting trends, but they are not foolproof in dealing with a significant other in one's life. We have to deal with people as individuals, giving attention to their differences. The key is to listen, to ask questions, and to communicate.

7. In Christian circles, how do you let a man or woman know you are valuable?

I have come to know hundreds of singles throughout my ministry. Some singles have clearly regarded themselves to be of great value and have projected well their sense of high self-worth. Other singles have projected their low self-worth equally clearly. How does it show? By how high that person's standards are.

For example, there was a man in one of the singles groups who was attractive, well-built, well off financially, a sincere Christian, and very sensitive. He was the man every woman wanted. He was asked out a lot by different women, but he consistently said no.

In that same group, there was a woman who was cute, petite, shapely. She had a soft and gentle spirit and was a committed Christian This woman was asked out by scores of men in the group, but she chose not to date either. It was no surprise who this man finally asked out on a date—the woman who had not dated indiscriminately. It was no surprise to me that she accepted a date with this man the first time he asked. They did not sell themselves cheaply to other people in the group. And by keeping themselves separate, by saving themselves emotionally and physically, they built this storehouse of emotional and personal wealth that everyone could sense.

People with high self-esteem will be attracted to each other. A man who understands the importance of sexual purity will be attracted to a woman who has that same understanding.

If you want to let others know of your value, don't let anyone treat you cheaply. That may mean not going out every night of the week, not engaging in flirtatious behavior, not dressing seductively, and not playing sexual games with many partners. I've known some men who like to kiss women even though they have no intention of a serious relationship, as well as women who like to kiss and hug on dates with no intention of ever dating that person again. When they do this, they are spending out of their moral account, and that will be noticed by others. The men who want the cheap thrill will be attracted to the "easy" women, but the men who are seeking more lasting relationships will not be attracted to them. And, of course, the opposite is also true: the women who have a high respect for their own self-worth and value will be attracted to men who have the same sense about themselves, and these women will not be attracted to men who treat other women cheaply.

Again, building up a sense of moral self-worth is exactly parallel to building financial worth. If we want to build up a savings account, we have to decide how much we will spend and how much we will save. We have to set up boundaries on what we use our money for.

In the same way, singles need to set up boundaries emotionally and personally in many different areas of life. For instance, it is inappropriate to tell deep personal secrets to every person you meet. A woman once told me how wonderful her date was the night before, because they stayed up all night and told each other all their deep personal secrets. She thought that was great, but I think that was dangerous. She had no boundaries. She was trusting him without discovering if he could be trusted or not. She did know how to protect her own moral value. Part of who she was as a person was her intimate past experiences, and to share that indiscriminately was to empty her moral bank account.

It reminds me of Hezekiah, one of the kings of Judah, allowing the emissaries from Babylon to look at all the royal jewels (2 Kings 20:12–19). He was boasting and showing off his wealth. He didn't have the wisdom to understand that once the rival king knew all that wealth was there, he would want it. Eventually the foreign king sent his armies to attack and to steal the wealth. Hezekiah had opened his boundaries and showed someone else his intimate goods without knowing whether the person could be trusted with that information or not. That happens often with singles. Remember, healthy boundaries usually communicate a sense of self-worth and value, just as a security fence around a home communicates wealth.

8. I feel that men more than women play the field and have lost the meaning of love and commitment. What do you think?

In my experience, both men and women have lost the meaning of love and the whole notion of moral purity as a foundation upon which to build their future lives. We each have a moral bank account, but both men and women alike have spent so freely that little if anything remains in their accounts. Success in life and a personal sense of self-worth come from making sure that we are making more deposits in that account than withdrawals. Some people never balance their checkbooks —they just hope they have enough and expect to bounce a check every once in a while. That's not a good way to handle finances. It's much better to monitor your bank account, have more deposits than withdrawals, and have good credit. The same is true in the moral arena.

9. Why do people have difficulty in making commitments?

As with the word *virgin,* the word *commit* has been twisted and has been seen in a negative light. *Commitment* is a positive term, but to a lot of people the word is regarded as the opposite of freedom. They feel it is an either/or situation—you can either be committed or be free. Actually, commitment frees us to have stability in our lives.

Why is commitment important in the value approach to sexuality? Because it is only in the context of commitments that people are able to develop relationships of lasting worth and value.

To return to our example of renting versus owning, people are free to choose to rent a place to live all of their lives. But if they sacrifice and save toward ownership of a house (which will require commitment and longevity), they will have something of great value in the long run. In the same way, appropriate commitments build value. It is only by committing ourselves to organizations, to causes, and to other persons that we find life to be of value. Lack of commitment does society and others no good. It is only through commitment that we can make lasting contributions.

10. Am I naive to believe that the Lord has one special man for me and that we will together build a marriage and lifelong commitment? If God does, how can I recognize this person?

Many Christian teachers believe that God has one particular person picked out for you; I do not agree. The reason people teach that is because their observation is from hindsight. (For an example of this, see Tim Stafford's, *Worth the Wait,* pp. 105–13, especially p. 107.)

People who deeply enjoy their marriage relationship cannot imagine receiving the same blessing from being married to someone else. They are looking back and saying, "My mate was God's perfect choice for me." I think that's romantic, but also problematic. First, the notion that God has already chosen a certain, specific person to be one's mate diminishes the role of personal choice and free will. Instead, it fosters the idea that each person must try to find God's perfect will in its absolute and inflexible specificity. Such singles end up as frustrated as the proverbial farm boy who had to search for a needle in a haystack.

Second, the idea that God has a perfect mate chosen for each person becomes twisted when the marriage goes sour. God then becomes the responsible party for choosing the mate, and the blame for the failed relationship is loaded upon God rather than on the individuals involved. If divorce follows, God may become the scapegoat.

God does not want us to act like children in this most important area of life; He doesn't want us to return to an ancient form of allowing others to choose someone for us to marry. Instead, He wants us to make wise decisions about whom we should marry, using our own resources and the wisdom and insight He has given us through godly counsel and the Word.

God is powerful enough to help us with whatever decision we make in this area. For those who are in difficult marriages, thinking that God has one special person for you offers a loophole. As one unhappily married woman said, "The real problem with our marriage is that he is not the perfect person God chose for me. I disobeyed God in marrying him, so there is no way I will be happy with him. I must divorce him to get back to the center of God's will."

That is absurd reasoning. We should not rationalize away a poor marriage. I once asked an unhappily married pastor's wife if she thought her husband was God's choice for her. She thought a moment and said, "Once you marry someone, that is God's choice for you. Before you marry, God has a lot of people whom He could shape to be your mate." I liked her response.

This notion of God's perfect mate also creates problems for those who lose a mate through death. One such widow said, "Jim was God's perfect choice for my life. I know there can never be anyone else for me. I hate being lonely, but I don't want to settle for second best. So I guess I'll stay single." Unfortunately, in doing so she is limiting the image of God from functioning fully in her life.

My wife and I have talked about what we each should do if the other was to die. I shared honestly that if by some tragic accident I were to lose my life, I would not want her to believe that the image of

God in her is so limited that she could not find happiness with someone else after my death. Although I have a wonderful relationship with my wife and am very grateful, I don't think I am the only person she could be happily married to, and vice versa.

The secret is not so much in looking for the perfect mate but in becoming a whole person who would make a great mate for someone. The more a single looks for someone else to provide completeness in his or her life, the more off the track he or she can get. Concentrate on developing a sense of personal wholeness and value. Quality friendships and relationships will follow.

11. Doesn't your whole paradigm of value and your $600 table illustration reduces sexuality to a commodity?

As with all metaphors and similes, the table story is not perfect. I do not want personhood to be seen as a mere commodity nor people to be objectified as possessions to be appraised. I try to say the opposite: because of the love of God shown in the sacrifice of Jesus Christ, people are priceless and can't be treated as commodities. The only reason I use this illustration is because most people have lost the ability to make moral and ethical decisions, but they are good at thinking in economic terms. Thus I use the illustration so that people can grasp more easily the much deeper truth that a person's sense of self-worth is directly related to how one allows oneself to be treated sexually.

The idea of using financial examples to communicate spiritual and relational truths actually is not original to me. It goes back to Jesus, who often used earthly illustrations to communicate deeper truths. He used an illustration about economics in the parable of the talents, communicating the deeper truth that our talents/gifts/abilities are to be used, not wasted or stored away (Matthew 25:14–30). He spoke of the need to count the cost before building a tower or going to war (Luke 14:25–35) and applied that financial lesson to the value of commitment in relationships, especially the commitment to follow God. The parables of the lost coin (Luke 15:8–10), the rich fool (Luke 12:13–21), the rich man and Lazarus (Luke 16:19–31), the unjust steward (Luke 16:1–13), the two debtors (Luke 7:41–50), the treasure and the pearl of great price (Matthew 13:44–46), and many others amply illustrate the appropriateness of economic analogies. But just because an analogy is appropriate, it does not follow that people should be viewed as commodities—any more than Jesus' analogy of the sheep and the goats should imply that people be treated as animals.

CHAPTER FOURTEEN

INCOMPATABILITY, ATTRACTIVENESS, AND SINGLE PARENTING

H ere are ten more questions single adults commonly ask about their sexuality and relationships with the opposite sex.

1. What about sexual incompatibility?

"My first marriage was a nightmare largely because of sexual incompatibility. When my marriage fell apart, I vowed that I would never get married again unless I found out first if my future partner and I were sexually compatible. Is it wrong of me to want to make sure?"

This woman caller on a radio program is similar to many singles. They want a guarantee that there will be no sexual problems in their marriage. One of the ways they seek the guarantee is to discover whether or not they are sexually compatible before marriage.

But the idea that a couple can discover sexual compatibility before marriage is a myth. Sex is not merely a mechanical process. Two people don't just fit together like a nut and a bolt or a foot in a shoe. That type of image depreciates what sex is all about. Good sex doesn't occur just because the parts fit easily. Sexual compatibility is a pilgrimage, a process. A couple has to journey down the road of compatibility because they have to deal with the history, the baggage, and the expectations that each person brings to the relationship.

A couple cannot deal with such adjustments in a short period of time. It takes years to develop sexual compatibility—and then only with hard work and communication. The idea that someone can "try on" lovers in the same way as trying on a shirt or a coat reveals a low view of sexuality.

Physiologically, the notion that "only one shoe will fit" is a myth. Remember the story of Cinderella? The prince had a glass slipper that only Cinderella's foot would fit. People are not like that, especially in the area of sex. God has created sex with incredible flexibility and variety. Sex is possible between people of all sizes, shapes, colors, and emotional makeup.

Before you kiss somebody, you don't worry if your lips are going to fit. Lips are amazingly flexible. Any two people who have the desire can work it out so they can kiss. The same is true for the rest of the body. God created our sexual apparatus with such amazing flexibility that men and women of any size and shape can find ways to be compatible sexually. Sex is possible even between people who are disabled.

Even if a man is impotent, he and his wife can be involved and fulfilled sexually. There may be certain acts that can't be performed, but the body has such diversity that a couple could still experience deep intimacy. A loving couple will work out their own compatibility rather than try to force their sexual relationship to fit some cultural norm.

Furthermore, sex is only one area of compatibility. In order to have a successful marriage, couples have to work out their relationship in several areas, such as financially, emotionally, and spiritually. If a man is a spender and the wife is a saver, the couple would have to work out compatibility in the financial area. But just because they are different in their financial habits and views does not mean they should not marry. It is as couples work out these compatibility issues that they cement their relationship and their intimacy becomes deeper. The same is true in the emotional area. If the woman is very emotional and the man resembles a robot, there will be incompatibility that will need to be worked out.

Sometimes it is these very differences that first brought the couple together. Opposites do attract. People are often attracted to each other because they are incompatible in some areas. The joy, the intensity, and the passion in their relationship sometimes come in discovering how to relate with another person and how to become one—in spite of the differences. In this regard relationships are like a puzzle. If the puzzle pieces are all similar, the puzzle will not hold together well. It is the distinctiveness in the pieces that adds to the strength of the puzzle.

The idea that a couple can discern before marriage whether they are compatible or not is a myth. There will be many areas of difference that they will discover after the marriage. The task then becomes making those differences become assets. With hard work and creativity, the couple can make the puzzle pieces fit and in the process strengthen the marriage even more.

Since the baby boomers in our culture are growing older, lots of new information is now surfacing about seniors and how active they are sexually. Often the seniors claim that sex is better for them than ever before. Why is that? Why are older people (even though not able to perform as well physically) more sexually fulfilled than younger people? It is because compatibility is a process. By loving and respecting each other over several years, a couple can develop sexual intimacy and depth that becomes so much more fulfilling than what is experienced in youth. We are not talking about a compatibility of body parts, but a compatibility of spirit and soul. The physical union is only a minor part of it.

2. What about couples that actually cannot have intercourse?

A woman wrote to me about a couple she knew who remained celibate before their wedding day. After their marriage, they discovered they had a physical problem; the man's penis was too large for the woman. "Sex is extremely uncomfortable and painful for them," the woman wrote. "The relationship is in trouble as a result. Doctors cannot help. Counseling was holding the line at best. Both believe that had they had premarital sex, this difficulty could have been avoided—even if it meant ending the relationship."

We sometimes think that the act of intercourse is necessary for sexual fulfillment. Not true. There are many ways a couple can bring pleasure to each other and communicate a sense of worth and value without intercourse.

Actually, every couple faces the possibility of living without sexual intercourse. People get sick, healthy bodies become disabled by accidents, and impotence and vaginal disorders do occur—all of which mean that intercourse sometimes is not possible. But an inability to perform intercourse does not mean that such a couple would be unable to find sexual fulfillment together. Adults that care for one another deeply can be sexual people together and experience profound intimacy without sexual intercourse.

Frankly, to question the wisdom of marriage simply on the basis of not being able to have intercourse suggests a shallow relationship. That reveals that they view intimacy in a limited way, that they have a superficial view of marriage, and that they have a lot to learn about the whole kaleidoscope of how God has created them.

Again, compatability is a process, not a starting point. Every couple will have issues to work through. If the couple doesn't have problems with penis size, they may have problems with lack of desire or too much desire, with fatigue or disease, with impotence or premature ejaculation, with honesty or deception, with fear or lack of trust. There are a million obstacles that could stand in the middle of any couple's road to fulfillment. And unfortunately, we aren't allowed to choose our obstacles in life. They just appear, and we have to deal with them or exit the road.

Obviously, true intimacy and closeness result when a couple learn that together they can face any obstacle—no matter how tough—and conquer it together. I would encourage the couple with the size problem to see it as a real opportunity for growth and strength. If they can navigate that problem, they will have the confidence to face anything in life and win.

3. Is sexual sin more devastating than any other? Is sexuality more important than other areas of life?

There are two extreme positions that are often taken regard sexual sin. One of them is that sexual sin is absolutely the worst thing that a person can do and is unforgiveable. I will never forget how, in a church youth group I worked with, one high school age teen struggled over this issue. It finally came out that he thought he had committed the unpardonable sin. He was too embarrassed to talk about it in public but told me later privately that the unpardonable sin he had committed was oral sex. He was convinced that what he had done was unforgiveable. The Bible does not say any one sexual act is unforgiveable, but instead talks about attitudes and motives. [1]

The other extreme is to say that sexual sins are not anything special and are weaknesses similar to cheating, overeating, or losing one's temper. Both extremes contain kernels of truth. Sexual sin is harmful (1 Corinthians 6:18–19), but sexual sin is also forgiveable. The correct answer lies somewhere in the middle of the two extremes.

During a seminar on single sexuality, a man in the audience responded to a panelist who said sexual sin is no different than losing one's temper. He said: "I have both lost my temper and committed sexual sin. And let me tell you from personal experience—sexual sin has been a lot of more damaging to my emotions and relationships than losing my temper. Expressing ourselves sexually involves our whole being. Because of this, to be used or misused in this area has serious results. I don't agree that you should mutually explore and decide what feels good for you, and if it feels good it's OK. *Two* people are involved in a sexual relationship, and it's much more complicated."

Though all actions in life have natural consequences, some have worse consequences than others. If I cut my finger with the sharp edge of a piece of paper, the consequences would be minor. But if I cut my finger with a chain saw, the consequences would be major. Sexual sins make deep wounds and leave terrible scars on the body and soul—wounds that are not easy to heal and scars that are not simple to get rid of. A person who has given up his or her purity finds it very difficult to feel pure again. There is hope, but the way back to value and purity in the sexual arena is not cheap or easy. It will require an extended period of celibacy.

Restoring value is similar to repaying a credit card debt. If I run up a bill of $100 on my credit card, it won't take long to pay off that debt. But if I run up a bill of thousands of dollars, it will take much longer to recover from that debt. Sexual sins leave a person more destitute than many other sins, so we need to take them more seriously. However, we must never forget that God's grace is sufficient for all. For most people, the problem is not being forgiven by God but learning to forgive self. I believe the key to feeling forgiven is to voluntarily undergo a period of sexual abstinence.

4. What role does being overweight play in our sexuality? What role does physical attractiveness, intelligence, and so on, play in our sexuality?

We all feel inadequate in some areas. Feeling inadequate is another obstacle on the road to relational intimacy. Inadequacies are a part of the challenge in relating. Being able to help another in spite of his or her inadequacies is a way of asserting the depth of a person's value and love.

Tennis partners, for example, both have strengths and certain weaknesses they use to help each other. One may be a better forehand player; the other a better backhand player. One might be stronger in serving; the other better at net play. Will they be able, in spite of their mutual inadequacies, to become championship players? Of course. The challenge of teamwork is accentuating the strengths and compensating for the weaknesses. Teams become champions in spite of their inadequacies and become better because those very inadequacies force them to work harder than those without weaknesses. Though less talented, they can become a better team. That's why the top singles tennis players often don't play doubles well, and why the best doubles teams are sometimes made up of mediocre singles players.

The same is true in relationships. Rather than thinking that our inadequacies disqualify us, we should look at them as a tool to make our relationships better and deeper.

That doesn't mean a person should not be concerned about his or her weight or hygiene or health, but it does mean that people can help each other improve in these areas. Tennis partners will help each other by practicing together to overcome weaknesses. If you struggle with being overweight, seek a friend to join you in your journey to lose weight. This does not mean using negative motivation such as berating, demeaning, or criticizing. It means setting goals, encouraging, and supporting one another. A loving, caring atmosphere must prevail.

We also need to realize that being overweight can be a way of insulating oneself from involvement with other people. It's similar to a king in a castle. One reason a king insists on huge stone walls, a moat, guards, and a drawbridge is the enemies who threaten his kingdom. If there were peace in the land, there would be no need for the walls or moat. Discord and strife naturally result in walls being constructed.

It is the same emotionally. When people discover that they have put up big walls in their lives, they need to find out why and seek to take them down, rather than withdraw and isolate themselves from relationships. Many times this type of discovery will help in the struggle of being overweight. When the walls start coming down, relationships become a priority, acceptance is found, and the weight problem takes care of itself.

5. What if my partner (though we are not married) makes me feel like a "billion dollars" sexually?

Ernest Hemingway was wrong when he said, "What is moral is what you feel good after and what is immoral is what you feel bad after."[2] Feelings are notoriously poor guides to truth and value. An example of this is extreme forms of sexuality, whose adherents claim moral correctness based on feelings. Certain activities "feel right" to the participants, even though the Bible (and sometimes society) sees them as immoral.

> Gay rights groups have made a political movement out of the "alternate lifestyle" of homosexual intercourse. There is a smaller but similar political movement in Britain called the Pedophilia Society, which lobbies for the rights of child molesters. A recent publication of a Christian theological group even had a kind word to say about beastiality.[3]

Clearly, value cannot be based merely on feelings. Yet people often feel of low value when in reality God has created them with great value. Conversely, a person can feel an exaggerated sense of self-importance, which may affect his/her behavior adversely.

Neither can we gauge relationships by feelings. For instance, if a couple lives together and one morning the man wakes up and says, "I feel married," that doesn't mean he is married. Or if a couple is married and one morning the wife wakes up and says, "I don't feel married anymore," that doesn't mean she is suddenly single. Feelings alone are not enough to convey the truth of a situation.

Once a young person discovers how to get a credit card, he could start spending and feel very rich. He would be enjoying all his toys and feel valuable, but in reality the value is negative because he has a huge debt. Sooner or later, the bills will come and the bankruptcy will become obvious; then reality hits. The same thing is true morally. A person can be bankrupt morally and not feel the results for a long time. A couple can be involved sexually and feel good about it for a while, but just because they *feel* good does not mean they are building a foundation for value that will last.

6. I always thought the Bible said that only sexual intercourse outside of marriage was wrong. That meant to me that "anything goes" except penetration. Now I'm confused. What's the Bible actually say?

The Bible nowhere actually says, "Thou shalt not have sexual intercourse before marriage." Instead, it tells us, "Flee sexual immorality" (1 Corinthians 6:18), and, "Neither let us commit fornication" (1 Corinthians 10:8, KJV). In both cases, the original word for immorality and fornication is the Greek word *porneia*, which has been translated in many other ways: whoredom, concubinage, adultery, incest, lewdness, uncleanness, and even symbolically as idolatry. Obviously, the word covers a wide range of actions and situations, usually including sexual intercourse outside of marriage, but is not limited to that.

It is interesting to note that the word *porneia* was a derivative of the classical Greek word *pernemi* and its root, *porn*, which meant to sell (especially slaves) and thus came to refer to a harlot who was for hire. Historically, some of the first prostitutes were in fact slaves. Prostitution grew with the increase in commerce and prosperity, since both male and female slaves were at the mercy of their masters' lusts.[3]

Porneia, then, has its roots in the idea of sex for sale, from which we get our word *pornography*. I would suggest that fornication, then, could be extended to include whenever one uses his or her sexuality to gain a profit or manipulate an outcome. If a woman uses her sexuality to control a man, I would call that a form of *porneia*. If a man withholds his sexuality to punish a woman, that too I would call *porneia*.

But even in its limited denotation, fornication has to mean more than just sexual intercourse. To pretend that anything up to penetration is acceptable for unmarried couples is to draw an arbitrary line. Clearly premarital sexual intercourse is prohibited in the Bible, but much more is meant to be included in that prohibition of fornication. The variety of ways in which the word *porneia* is used in the Scriptures requires a broader definition of fornication.

7. What about the tendency of our culture to desensitize us to moral values? If some people can live immorally and not feel guilty, will the value or worth really depreciate for them?

It is easy to deceive ourselves. Some people live their entire lives on credit. They never learn the lesson that they can't keep borrowing forever. I know of one couple who continued to rent homes far beyond their means. The family would move or be evicted frequently, which would embarrass the children terribly. The parents acted wealthy, but in reality they weren't. As a result, the children suffered and lived in daily fear that their secret poverty would be discovered. That is not a good way to live.

In a similar way, there are couples who are extending themselves sexually until they are way over their heads morally. Sooner or later, they will have to pay the price. The emotional bill for multiple abortions will come due. The social bills for having sex with many partners will come due. One partner may never be able to be satisfied sexually in a monogamous relationship because of former sexual conduct. The spiritual bills for denying God's wisdom and direction will come due. Sometimes the bills for sexual conduct come due when a person gets married and has children. Whatever the case and whenever it happens, if you spend on credit, sooner or later the bill will come due.

But the issue is deeper than just pragmatics. There is also an important ethical issue at stake here. It is the need for an objective standard for morality. Right and wrong cannot be decided by what feels right. Just because an action feels good, it does not follow that it therefore is the right thing to do. It may feel good to overeat, to get drunk, or to do drugs, but in each case harm can result. In spite of the words in some current songs or what "free thinkers" may say, feeling good or feeling like a billion dollars does not make an action right morally. Adolf Hitler no doubt felt good about his early successes in World War II. In fact, he said, "Success is the sole earthly judge of right and wrong." Hopefully, even today's free thinkers would disagree with Hitler on this point, and in doing so, would agree with the poverty of the "it feels good" approach.

8. What about singles who won't ever marry?

The idea of celibacy helping a person retain a sense of self-worth may be seen by some as just another way of saying, "Save yourself until marriage." But what about the person who will never marry?

The main issue I have been emphasizing is not "saving yourself until marriage." Instead, temporary celibacy for single adults is a positive way to assert, build, and protect their self-worth. Whether such a valuable single decides to marry or not, he or she will possess a deep sense of self-worth and physical value. Regardless of whether a person marries or not, living a life of sexual purity to protect and assert one's self-worth will enable that single person to feel a deep sense of personal value, which is essential to one's well being and fulfillment. The issue is "save yourself so you will be convinced and assured of your own value, regardless of whether or not you marry."

9. Do you think youth are as sexually active today as they have been in the past, and is this why in biblical times marriage occurred when they were so young?

Morality in ancient times is an issue of debate. Some sociologists and archeologists believe that prehistoric tribes were very sexually active and very clannish or communal. Others disagree vehemently and say they were monogamists and exclusive in their sexuality. You can pretty much pick whatever view you want to believe.

I believe that the further you go back in civilization and relationships, the more complex the relationships were. It has been shown through a study of African tribes that their clannish rules and rituals were complex—much more involved than they are now. Personally, I think that in prehistoric times, or in ancient biblical times, people were not as sexually active as they are today.

However, divorce was more common in biblical times than it is now. Pliny the Younger wrote a letter in which he mentioned a man who was going through his twenty-fourth divorce. You have to remember, though, that they also had multiple wives.

10. I'm a single parent. I have struggled with how to teach my kids about sex, but I also feel like a hypocrite because I haven't been perfect in that area myself. How can I help them?

I think a letter I received from a single woman we will call Jenny best answers this question. Jenny's parents warned her to date little, monitored her social life closely, and would not talk about sex or her fears. As an adult, Jenny felt embarrassed and unqualified to teach her children. Jenny's words show there is hope.

I have felt at a loss to teach my children "why" and have to admit that I also have this "fear" that my parents modeled. I have felt inadequate to discuss sexuality with them and always wonder if I'm doing or saying the right thing.

When I came home from the seminar, I actually cried for hours—thinking back to my teenage years. I was grieving the loss of not being told how valuable I was and not being treated with love and respect. I was grieving the fact that things weren't explained and I wasn't trusted. I was grieving because I wanted different parents . . . parents who expressed their love for me in spiritual ways and taught me about God and His love for me. The taffeta dresses and patent leather shoes were nice, but they were not lasting. . . .

I ask God to help me change that pattern—to give me a deeper understanding—and to give my daughter that feeling of value and the strength to say, "No, I choose to wait until after marriage. I choose God's way because I know it is best for me and whether I marry or not, I will still have my own sense of self-worth."

This woman took the correct first step toward teaching her child about sex and value—she faced squarely her past and began to work though her own issues. Then, once she had a new base of personal value and a sense of sexual worth, she was able to begin teaching her daughter the same things. Of course, that is just the start. She then will need to follow through those lessons with congruent actions and a pure lifestyle. She will have to live out what she says. And her daughter will be watching every move, listening to every word, sensing every attitude—wondering all the time if this approach to sex and value really works. Is her mother really happier this way? Or does she get angry, depressed, and moody more often?

If their sexuality is approached with honesty and confidentiality, she and her daughter can learn the lessons together. What a great opportunity! Their learning process can become a great journey for a mother and daughter to make together. They can benefit from one another's experiences, can talk through their failures and frustrations, and make and keep commitments to one another. A college student told me that she was happy that during her teenage years her mother was single rather than married. Since this was not the usual perspective, I asked her why she had felt that way. Her response was heartwarming.

"It's not a problem for me now, but when I first started being attracted to boys and then started dating, I was really confused. Some people were telling me that sex was no big deal, and others were saying that I shouldn't do it. All my friends' parents said it was wrong, but we knew it was easy for them to say that—they were married. But when my mom told me that she had sexual desires too, but still said no to sex, it really made me pay more attention to her suggestions.

"She was going through the very same things I was. When she came home from a date, I asked her about it. I even asked her if they kissed or whatever. She gave me honest answers. Then we talked about why it was better to not get too physical before marriage. When I came home from a date, she asked me too."

Then this woman added, "My mom is my best friend. We can talk about anything. I did miss my dad, but having a single mom really helped me."

Since single parents and single teens both have to deal with loneliness, finances, sexuality, dating, love, romance, betrayal, and many other issues especially relevant to singles, they share a common bond that married parents and teens just don't have. Of course, not every single parent and child may end up best friends, but they can use their unique relationship as a bridge for close communication. If single parents deal with their own sexuality in a positive way, they can powerfully influence their children to a healthy and whole sexuality.

CHAPTER FIFTEEN

MASTURBATION, FANTASIES, AND LUST

We conclude with answers to three questions unmarried teens and adults often think about but only occasionally ask. What about masturbation? What about fantasies? What about lust? My answers to these questions are again based on the all-important principle of value—value that builds self-worth for ourselves and for others.

ABOUT MASTURBATION

"What about masturbation?" is by far the most common question asked by singles—when they are allowed to write down questions anonymously. In seminars I have conducted, this question is asked four times as often as any other. Of course, this only happens if the anonymity is authentic. If anonymity is not respected and/or the question and answer time is oral, the question may not be asked at all. This is because it takes an exceptionally gutsy single adult to ask publicly about masturbation.

In polite society, masturbation is one of the unmentionables that has no place in social conversation. And yet many studies show that sexual self stimulation is a common practice among single adults. (Masturbation is not just an adolescent issue, as Smedes seems to imply in his discussion of "self-petting" in *Sex for Christians,* pp. 160–64.) McCary argued in his book *Human Sexuality* that 95 percent of men and between 50 and 90 percent of women masturbate.[1] If the figures are accurate, almost all men and most women masturbate at some time in their single lives.

Harold Ivan Smith, in a gutsy and informative address to the National Association of Single Adult Leaders in 1992 in San Francisco, said that although the famous but dated Kinsey Report found that 92 percent of males and 58 percent of females masturbated at some point in their lives, more recent studies have reported the figures at 97 percent and 83 percent, respectively.

Smith also noted that one recent study showed that among senior citizens over age eighty, 72 percent of males and 40 percent of females masturbate. Smith's numbers represent the percentages of all adults that masturbate, so it would naturally follow that the percentages for single adults would be higher.

Smith refers as well to a recent study of 312 single adults, 98 percent of whom identified themselves as Christians active in a large single adult ministry in a metropolitan area. Of these adults, consisting of a 40/60 split between men and women and almost half college graduates, 75 percent admitted to having masturbated within the last month and 52 percent within the last week.[2] Of these church-going Christians, only 6 percent believed masturbation to be morally wrong. Though the study does not indicate how many singles masturbate on a regular basis, these findings suggest masturbation is a more common in the Christian community than many evangelical leaders admit.

The widespread practice represents a major change in attitudes regarding masturbation, and so a brief history is in order.[3] For most of Western history, society and the church have warned against the practice. This was probably expressed most strongly by the medieval theologian Thomas Aquinas, who said that since every ejaculation that could not lead to procreation was sinful, masturbation was a sin "worse than intercourse with one's own mother." Of course, not everyone felt as strongly negative about masturbation as Aquinas. There have always been advocates on both sides of the issue, just as there are today.

However, in England during the Enlightenment, the negative view of masturbation became even stronger. In 1640, Richard Capel, the preacher of Magdalen College in Oxford, which was the center of Puritan teaching, claimed that "self-pollution" was the greatest sin against nature and led to bodily weaknesses, impotence, and shortening of the lifespan because of suicide. A Puritan physician named Bekker believed that the vice of masturbation was widespread among both men and women, and he felt obliged as a doctor to be frank about its consequences. Those consequences, he wrote, ranged from vomiting and weakening of the organs to backaches, attacks of rage, and epilepsy.[4]

Bekker's book unleashed a torrent of publicity. The book was translated into many languages and published in many editions. Almost fifty years later the crusade against masturbation reached its pinnacle when a Swiss physician, Simon-Andre Tissot, published his book *Onan, A Treatise on the Diseases Produced by Onanism.* "Onanism" was the label Bekker had used to describe masturbation, claiming that Onan of Judah (in Genesis 38) practiced masturbation. (In truth, Onan simply refused to culminate a sexual union with his brother's widow, as required by Jewish law. Onan spilled his seed on the ground in an act of *coitus interruptus.)* Tissot claimed masturbation, or onanism, had such after-effects as deteriorating brain size.

Fortunately, today these myths and their corresponding remedies have been medically debunked. On a popular level, although masturbation is still generally considered to be unacceptable, it has become more acceptable in the past twenty years. As one single woman told me, "I was really surprised about all the questions about masturbation. I was told it was OK by my parents and grew up thinking that everyone did it. I can't believe that so many single Christians are so hung up about it."

For this woman, the issue is simple. But for many single adults who were raised before the sexual revolution, or for those—regardless of age—who were taught the sinfulness of masturbation, the whole subject is quite confusing and frustrating. Christian singles at different seminars have asked me the "M" question in many ways: "Is masturbation a permitted or scriptural activity for sexual release?" "Is masturbation a sin in God's eyes?" "What is the truth in 'use it or lose it?'" "A good friend once said to me, 'If you don't have sugar, use a substitute.' What do you think?'"

Before we answer these questions, consider the stories of two individuals, Penny and Patrick. Penny, twenty-six, says she has "never been sexually active," but she qualifies that statement by adding, "I have never experienced nor participated in intravaginal sex, anal sex, or oral sex."

Penny wrote in her sexual history that she considers herself "very strict and very strong with [her sexual] boundaries." But as a seventh grader, she remembers the influence of her sister, one year older than she: "My sister was very promiscuous and physical with her boyfriends, especially one in particular. They would sneak over to our house when Mom was gone and would 'make out' heavily. There are a couple of things I saw that really upset me, but out of a 'pact' with my sister about being a good sister and keeping secrets, I never really told my mom the whole picture of what was going on, but I did give her some hints. This excessive physicalness led to my sister's pregnancy. She gave the child up for adoption."

As a result of her sister's actions, Penny felt both curiosity about boys and fear that sexual feelings were dangerous. Out of her curiosity, one night in her bedroom about a year later, "I experimented 'touching' myself in the genital area and discovered that it really felt good. That began what I consider an 'on and off' habit of masturbating.

"Over the period of years to the present time, my desire and urge to masturbate was inconsistent. However, when I became 'born again' as a sophomore in high school, this became a source of great anxiety for me and still is. I was taught in church that masturbation is a 'sin.' Each time I indulged in that behavior, I felt terribly ashamed and guilty. But then, after being taught and reading that masturbation is normal and healthy and isn't something dirty, I could 'rationalize' my behavior and not feel bad about doing it.

"The problem is I'm not sure if the behavior is sinful. Am I feeling guilty because the Holy Spirit is convicting me? Or do I feel guilty because that is what I have been taught? It's a tough call. I am trying not to indulge that behavior, but I find that the older I get and the more stimulated and curious I get about sex, the more I feel better about releasing my sexual tension and exploring my sexuality through masturbation—because it is 'safe' for me and my boundaries can remain intact. Yet I feel guilty. . . . I have not resolved this issue."

Since then, Penny has allowed boyfriends to have little physical contact with her—only a little kissing and hand-holding. Once she allowed a boyfriend of five years to touch her breasts. "I figured, why not? It might be fun, and I knew I wasn't in danger of getting too excited with him," she explained. "It was the only time I ever allowed anyone to get physical with me."

But as a result she concluded, "I feel like in the future such physicalness will only be appropriate in my marriage. I only want my husband to have the privilege of caressing me. I want to give my intimate parts only to my husband."

Then Penny added, "Your 'value' approach to sex is very appropriate and right on target. This approach to celibacy is not a new concept to me. It is one I have operated from. I do consider myself valuable and consider 'celibacy' to be valuable and something that should be treasured, honored, respected, and desired. I feel that our own virginity is a gift that God enables us to have and is one of the most important gifts that we can give our spouses."

This single woman has been able to develop a healthy view of both sexuality and celibacy, and she is able to appreciate how it affects her sense of personal value. But in spite of all this, masturbation is still a troublesome issue for her. She feels both good and guilty about it, and she has heard confusing messages from friends and spiritual leaders.

Penny still has a way to go on her journey toward sexual wholeness and integration, but I think she is far ahead of most of her peers, as is illustrated by Patrick. A single adult, Patrick discovered masturbation at age sixteen while looking at pictures from a swimsuit issue of *Sports Illustrated.*

His response to his action? "I was quite shocked. I was raised in a very strict and fundamentalistic religious environment, and I lacked any real support. I tried to tell my step-father, but he only sought to punish me. I didn't realize what effect masturbation could have on me, and it wasn't too long before I did it again. I somehow felt strange about myself and guilty too. My stepfather sought to make me quit by letting others in authority in our church know about my problem."

Patrick bemoaned the fact that he received little support or help from those around him. "And certainly not any accurate information. Somehow, I lived in a world of guilt for much of my adolescence. I didn't really date in high school and only began to date when I went to a nearby junior college. To this day, I have maintained my virginity in the technical sense and have had little sexual contact with girls. But when I was growing up, I knew my friends were sexually active. Somehow I avoided that, and while I am glad to this day, it still has left me with other problems.

"I still masturbate—not so much for some faceless person focusing on a single body part but out of imagining someone warm and loving. I feel pretty lonely and isolated. Nowadays, I don't beat myself up with a lot of guilt over it like I used to. I do my best to steer clear from masturbation and any stimulation that would lead me to masturbate. However, I still slip up and do it. I do my best to claim God's forgiveness and to repent of it, and not to dwell on it or let it make me depressed. That would be an endless cycle. . . .

"Once people know that I am still a virgin, they applaud my 'staying power' and congratulate me. However, I grew up in an environment where even the young Christian kids around me were sexually active. This had the effect of making me feel very inadequate, and it is a feeling I still need to fight to this day. . . . My big concern is that I will not be sexually adequate for women. I am not a stud nor do I have this great physique. It is hard to imagine a woman wanting me sexually . . . actually I don't worry about this much . . . I for one will press on. I would really hate to think I could be single all my life, and I certainly don't want this gift from God."

IS MASTURBATION OK?

So is masturbation OK for single Christians, or is it a sin? Many different answers are given to this question, just as there are different approaches to the whole issue of sexuality. Let me list just a few of the statements that have been made by prominent Christian teachers and theologians. I am indebted to Harold Ivan Smith for the following references, but I will list these statements without mentioning names or references. I do this for a reason: I have known many Christian singles who are unduly swayed by certain personalities that are popular today. They will agree with what an authority figure says, rather than closely investigating what he or she said.

Most of the statements oppose the practice; a few see the action as neutral, neither right nor wrong.

- "Masturbation is sin. The alternatives are clear—self control or marriage. There is no third option. It constitutes a perversion of the sex act."
- "Masturbation is an unnatural way of dealing with the sex drive; it's second-rate sex."
- "It's my opinion that masturbation is not much of an issue with God. It is a normal part of adolescence which involves no one else. I'm not telling you to masturbate, and I hope you won't feel the need for it. But if you do, it is my opinion that you should not struggle with guilt. The best I can do is suggest that you talk to God personally about it."
- "Masturbation brings inevitable, though typically mild, guilt. I suspect it's because every adolescent brain is able to reflect, 'I know I was made for something better than this.'"
- "Masturbation is a practice best avoided by Christian young people. There is no biological need to masturbate."
- "We do not feel it is an acceptable practice for Christians. It violates 1 Corinthians 7:9, 'It is better to marry than to burn.'"
- "It is a phase enroute to a better way of sexual fulfillment. It is not morally wrong, but neither is it personally sufficient. It is not on the same casual level as other activities, but neither is it a terribly secret sin."
- "The act of masturbation in and of itself is neither good nor evil, but it can be, for a Christian, a peg upon which one hangs his guilt and anxieties. It is time we stopped making such a big deal out of masturbation."
- "It's satanic, carnal, opposed to the best interests of people committed to the Lord. It wouldn't damn your soul, but it would limit your health. It's a rejection, not a release, of self discipline."

A few commentators see masturbation as positive, a release valve for sexual pressure. It is even "a gift from God," according to one commentator:

- "When masturbation is used solely as an occasional, limited means of sexual self control until marriage, it is within the Christian understanding of God's plan for the purpose of young men's lives."
- "For those without partners, masturbation can be that occasional gift through which we are graced to break through the sexual dualisms that beset and alienate us."
- "Masturbation is generally wrong. It's sin when the only motive is sheer pleasure. It's sin when it becomes a compulsive habit. It's sin when the habit results from inferior feelings. But it can be right when used as a limited temporary program of self-control to avoid lust. Masturbation used in moderation without lust for the purpose of retaining one's purity is not immoral."
- "Masturbation can be a positive factor in your total development. It is a gift from God."

If you feel confused by all the opinions, then you can better understand the quandary singles face on this issue. Basically, there are three common views: two extremes and one middle of the road. One extreme says masturbation is a abomination in God's eyes and always wrong. On the other extreme is the notion that is gaining more and more popularity—that masturbation is a positive expression for both singles and marrieds. One author says it's God's gift to single adults, another says that it is one of the keys to successful singlehood. The "middle of the road" school says that it is sometimes bad and sometimes OK, depending on such factors as frequency and purpose.

Is masturbation something that should be avoided by Christian single adults, or is it the key to loving oneself in a healthy way? I think a helpful answer will be structured in terms of the whole paradigm of value and self worth. The question has to be, "Does masturbation enhance or inhibit the purpose of our single sexuality, which is to protect and assert a sense of personal and physical value?" To put it simply, is a person devalued by the practice of masturbation? If masturbation diminishes a person's sense of self-worth, it will inhibit his or her ability to develop relationships that are founded on a mutual sense of value.

Controlled masturbation might be like a small withdrawal from one's savings account. If too many withdrawals are made, or if nothing is ever deposited to the account (as when masturbation becomes an uncontrollable and obsessive desire), the sense of personal worth and value will diminish. A person who feels devalued in this way will tend to isolate himself/herself from others and withdraw from relationships. I think masturbation in this sense would be harmful.

The bottom line is singles must be honest with themselves about what part masturbation has in their lives. Does it build or destroy their sense of personal value? Is there a great deal of withdrawing from the moral bank account, or is it making self control possible so that the person is saving himself/herself morally. I don't claim that considering how masturbation affects the sense of personal worth is easy. But I do think singles understand this economics analogy better than they understand the measurements of frequency and purpose, so they are more apt to apply the concept better.

If masturbation is occasionally OK to control one's sexual urges, we must also ask, "Just how often may a single masturbate? Once a year? Once a month? Once a week? Once a day?" Any attempt to draw a line will be arbitrary, so this factor is limited in its helpfulness. Some would say that the purpose is most important: "Is your purpose to be able to control one's sexual urges or to give yourself pleasure?" Some authors argue that the first purpose is acceptable, whereas the second is not. But how can someone differentiate between the two? We seem to be thrown back on the problem that confronted Johann von Wesel: masturbation is acceptable if we don't enjoy it too much.

What about masturbation in marriage? Just as genital intimacy is considered appropriate in marriage, so masturbation for intimacy and upholding value is permissible in marriage. However, even in marriage masturbation can be helpful or detrimental. Mutual masturbation can be a beneficial asset as an alternative to intercourse in marriage, or it can be detrimental if it becomes an isolated activity that causes a distancing between the partners or causes one or both to feel devalued.

IS MASTURBATION SIN?

The Bible says nothing about masturbation. The passage in the Old Testament about Onan who spilled his seed on the ground has nothing to do with masturbation. But Onan's action says much about how we are to treat others and that we are valuable in God's sight. Furthermore, it instructs us to live in such a way as to protect and cherish that value, rather than destroying it. Masturbation that makes us feel out of control—or seeking control—does not preserve our value as sexual beings.

But how can singles build up a sense of value and self-worth? Let's recall our lesson in chapter 3 about about King David: building up a reservoir of value will involve sacrifice. It has to cost us something. As Donald Goergen wrote in *The Sexual Celibate,*

> Celibate love forgoes genital sexuality in order to be single for Christ. If one is going to be interpersonally free as a single person, genital abstinence contributes to this goal. The celibate struggles to forgo genital love in his interpersonal life and thus to transcend experiencing genitality as a need. Masturbation, however, is genital activity. For this reason, it is something that a celibate person wants to grow beyond. As genital activity . . . [masturbation] represents the fact that a celibate has not fully outgrown his need for genital expression, which he or she is choosing to outgrow. Masturbation, for the celibate . . . falls short of the ideal.[5]

ARE FANTASIES SIN?

I chose to deal with the issue of fantasies following the question about masturbation because the issues and solution are much the same. Again, there are two extremes—the view that fantasies are actually a gift from God for single adults, and the view that to fantasize is to commit a terrible sin that must be conquered at all costs. There also is a middle view that admits the dangers and allows some positive benefits.

Both ancients and moderns agree, there is a way to fantasize and not sin, just as there is a way to masturbate and not sin. The basic issue is: is your fantasy taking advantage of or objectifying some specific person? Jesus said, "Anyone who looks at a woman lustfully has already committed adultery with her in his heart" (Matthew 5:28). I think He was careful in His choice of words and was meaning a specific woman. To fantasize about a romantic sunset or a candlelight dinner with a faceless stranger may not be sin. To think of a non-descript person in sexual terms, such as imagining what it would feel like to be kissed, to imagine what it feels like to be held (even wrap your own arms around yourself to feel the sensation) may not be sinful. This is not to imply that all kissing or holding is positive. Even kissing or embracing can be a devaluing experience.

The dividing line between an appropriate and an inappropriate fantasy is whether or not the fantasy motivates a person to relate to others or causes the person to withdraw from others. If a person would rather sit and fantasize than relate to real people, such fantasizing is harmful. If the activity becomes obsessive and isolates a person, there is an even greater danger. In both cases, the image of God in us, the drive to love and be loved, is hindered.

However, if a person uses fantasy as a way of controlling impulses, such activity is positive and can enhance relationships. This is especially true for a person who has a difficult time with physical control when dating.

In addition, a person who chooses to fantasize frequently may develop a private fantasy life that is easier than dealing with real people in relationships. That's why some people get hooked on pornography. The women and men models in the pictures never refuse the reader. They are readily available, they don't argue or reject anyone, they don't have personality problems that need to be dealt with. Excessive fantasies and/or pornography (like homosexuality) are an easy way out, a cop-out, an escape from doing a real work in real relationships with real people. He or she can escape reality intentionally, short-circuiting intended relationships or believing lies in a make-believe world.

Why would singles choose to avoid relationships and sink into the world of obsession? Perhaps because of pain from their past, they feel that the risk of relating is just too much. Or others might do it because they have failed in relationships so many times and can't stand the thought of failing again. Another person might choose to retreat into that world because of deep feelings of inferiority. But this fantasy world is more destructive than helpful. Obsessive fantasies cause people to retreat and be isolated, instead of motivating people to do the work of relationships and learn to love and forgive real people. Rather than allowing the image of God to be developed fully within, such fantasies prevent the image of God from being actualized.

The obsessions also can lead a person in a downward spiral toward increased isolation. They can become sexual black holes that suck everything out of a person and lead to feelings of devaluation. Because God has designed us to be with people, isolation or withdrawal is destructive to the personhood and potential God created in each human. The end result, not surprisingly, is a devalued sense of self and sexuality.

HOW CAN I CONTROL LUST?

That lust is sin is clear from Jesus' declaration during His Sermon on the Mount. Lust is a form of adultery (Matthew 5:28). It is always destructive, always devaluing. And it is a powerful force, once we choose to pay it attention. In *Godric*, Frederick Buechner's novel about a twelfth-century holy man, the main character happens to see his sister Burcwen bathe. Rather than calling out to her and announcing his presence, he watched from a distance:

Within my mind she stands there yet. Her naked limbs are shapely. Her virgin breasts are pale and soft as doves. Her hair is bright with sun. She stoops to cup some water in her hand. Susanna never bathed more chaste and fair than she, all unaware that not far off the hidden elders looked on her with lust.

Lust is the ape that gibbers in our loins. Tame him as we will by day, he rages all the wilder in our dreams by night. Just when we think we're safe from him, he raises up his ugly head and smirks, and there's no river in the world flows cold and strong enough to strike him down.[6]

Lust indeed is a powerful animal. But it is not a free, independent animal. It is a parasite that can live only off the lives of others. Like a leech that sucks dry the blood of its host, lust will destroy the very life it attaches itself to. It is a dangerous foe, worthy of the greatest fear and respect. Singles should be careful in the presence of this monster, lest they too become victims in its long path of destruction.

Though lust is terrible and voracious, it is not automatic. It can be fought. It can even be conquered. One can be tempted and not give in to the temptation. Lust is not all-powerful. Neither is to lust the same action as to fantasize. One can lust without fantasizing, and vice versa.

Both Jesus in Matthew 6 and James in James 1 seem to suggest that there is a moral space, or period of time, between the temptation of sin and the act of sin. Being tempted to sin doesn't mean a person has sinned. A man can look upon a woman and be sexually tempted and not lust. A woman can look on a man and be sexually tempted and yet not sin. In that moral space we can make a choice to act out that temptation or not act it out.

In chapter 6, I made the suggestion that every sexually tempting situation is a call to prayer. That is just one option; there are others. The point is that when we are tempted, we are at a crossroads. We can choose to follow the temptation, or we can choose an alternative route—one that respects and enhances our sense of personal worth and value. Therefore, a person can be sexually tempted and yet refrain from lusting.

Smedes helpfully points out this difference:

It is foolish to identify every erotic feeling with lust. There is a sexual desire that feels like a lonely vacuum yearning to be filled, a longing for intimacy that broods unsettled in one's system. To identify this as lust is to brand every normal sexual need as adultery. Eros, the longing for personal fulfillment, must not be confused with lust, the untamed desire for another's body. Nor is every feeling of attraction toward an exciting person the spark of lust. It would be odd indeed if the Creator put attractive people in the world and forbade us to notice them. But there is a difference between the awareness of someone's sexual attractions and being dominated by a desire for that person's body.[7]

WHAT ABOUT SEXUAL ADDICTIONS?

We have warned earlier about the devaluing consequences of fantasies that become obsessive. Thus single and married people alike ask how they can control their fantasies. "What about sexual addictions caused by obsessive fantasies? Would twelve-step programs or support groups for addictions be helpful?"

For some people, support groups might be very helpful. Many people have been greatly helped by such groups as Alcoholics Anonymous and Narcotics Anonymous. But such groups should be viewed as temporary helps, to be abandoned once the necessary sense of personal value and strength has been acquired. If a support group becomes a permanent fixture, the individual has just replaced one addiction with another. The group may be a more socially acceptable addiction than a chemical one, but it is still an addiction. In the same way, a self-help group for sexual addiction can provide a temporary help in conquering this problem.

In other cases, though, such groups can actually become harmful. Sexual addicts may become aroused by the discussion. In that case, the group would present an opportunity for the addiction to flourish rather than find healing. It would be like going to an AA meeting and having alcohol for refreshments. Second, these groups, if not completely and confidentially led, may actually give sexual addicts the opportunity to connect with others who have the same problem. It would be like putting gasoline on a fire.

There is a way to find release from this quagmire, which also works for those who are obsessive about masturbation. It is the same plan that was offered earlier in chapter 11 to help couples back off from sexual involvement. The same practical steps discussed there also apply here: (1) acknowledge the problem, (2) make a plan, (3) work the plan, (4) have an accountability partner, (5) undergird all with prayer.

An especially helpful resource in this area is a short article in the fall 1982 *Leadership Journal* called "The War Within: An Anatomy of Lust," The article generated the most mail to the editors of any article printed in the magazine, and it continues to be rated in reader surveys as one of the most helpful articles ever. It is the amazingly honest and shocking story of a minister's struggle with lust, pornography, and sexual deviance, and also chronicles his road back to balance and sexual healing. I recommend it enthusiastically.

The anonymous author describes how after ten years of struggle with lust and sexual addictions, and after almost a thousand prayers for forgiveness and deliverance, his prayers were finally answered and the monster was conquered. Central to the healing process was an insight gained from reading *What I Believe,* by Francois Mauriac. Mauriac denies that the common reasons offered for sexual purity are sufficient. He too decries the reasons as all negative and, as such, lacking the power to propel us to victory in this crucial arena. "Most of our arguments for purity are negative arguments: be pure, or you will feel guilty, or your marriage will fail, or you will be punished."

Instead, Mauriac concludes that there is only one positive way to combat lust. The author describes it this way:

> Mauriac concludes that there is only one reason to seek purity. It is the reason Christ proposed in the Beatitudes: "Blessed are the pure in heart, for they shall see God." Purity, says Mauriac, is the condition for a higher love—for a possession superior to all possessions, God Himself.
>
> The thought hit me like a bell rung in a dark, silent hall. So far, none of the scary, negative arguments against lust had succeeded in keeping me from it. Fear and guilt simply did not give me resolve; they added self-hatred to my problems. But here was a description of what I was missing by continuing to harbor lust: I was limiting my own intimacy with God. The love He offers is so transcendent and possessing that it requires our faculties to be purified and cleansed before we can possible contain it. [8]

I wholeheartedly agree with this author. Negative reasons for sexual purity are simply not powerful enough to protect and motivate single adults in today's world. Nor are they adequate to usher singles into an experience of the joy that Jesus claimed to be able to give. Negative reasons only protect from punishment. They are empty and have no actual content with which singles can fill their lives. Singles who try to maintain purity based on negative reasons alone may maintain purity, but that purity will be vacuous.

Positive reasons for single celibacy, however, do much more than just guard against impurity and destruction. They have solid, genuine content. They fill up a single person and provide a deep sense of satisfaction such as one feels after an exceptionally healthy and hearty meal.

The positive side of single sexuality allows us both to obey God and to experience the pleasure of purity. In addition, it enables us as single adults to develop a solid foundation for lives of self-worth and value, which in turn brings in a deep sense of joy and contentment. We experience what can be called pure joy!

NOTES

Chapter 1: Can Singles Thank God For Sexuality?

1. See Joan Timmerman, "Thank God It's Tuesday! A Positive Theology of Sexuality," cassette recording, 1982 (tapes are unavailable); and Reay Tannahill, *Sex in History* (New York: Stein and Day, 1980), 146.

Chapter 3: Why Do Singles Sometimes Feel Worthless?

1. Carolyn See, "The New Chastity," *Cosmopolitan* (November 1985), 382.
2. Ibid., 383.

Chapter 4: God's Surprising Answer—The Value of Sexuality

1. Colin Brown, ed. *New International Dictionary of New Tesament Theology*, vol. 3 (Grand Rapids: Zondervan, 1986), 1,071.

Chapter 5: Does Sex Guarantee Intimacy?

1. Reay Tannahill, *Sex in History* (New York: Stein and Day, 1980), 423–24.
2. R. J. Levin, "The End of the Double Standard?" *Redbook*, October 1975, 38.
3. Barna and Associates, "Executive Report: The 'Why Wait' Church Teen Sexuality Survey" (Dallas: Josh McDowell Ministry, 1987), 1, 5–6.
4. George N. Cornell, "Consistency Seems to Rule Political, Doctrinal Beliefs," Associated Press News Service, 28 February 1992.
5. Jon Nordheimer, "Sex, Lies, and Consequences," New York Times News Service, 4 March 1992.
6. Scott Peck, *The Road Less Traveled* (New York: Simon & Schuster, 1978), 19.

Chapter 7: The Hidden Purpose Behind Single Sexuality

1. Scott Peck, *The Road Less Traveled*, 90.
2. Lewis Smedes, *Sex for Christians* (Grand Rapids, Eerdmans, 1976), 32–33
3. Ibid., 34.
4. Peter Brown, *The Body and Society* (New York: Columbia Univ., 1988), 169.
5. Ibid., 160–77.

Chapter 8: How to Handle Temptation

1. Lewis Smedes, *How Can It Be All Right When Everything Is All Wrong?* (San Francisco: Harper & Row, 1982), 109.

Chapter 9: Should Sexual Intimacy Increase With Commitment?

1. Walter Trobisch, *I Married You* (*London:* InterVarsity, 1971), 96–97.

2. Though the chapter "Sexuality and Singles" offered a clear (though unoriginal) overview of a few of the basic sexual issues facing singles, I was very disappointed in one regard. In a book inspired by the monastic vows, Foster did not draw at all on the whole history of the monastic experience with single celibacy. What a gold mine of literature and case studies he could have marshaled to illustrate the value of single celibacy. Surely the rich history of celibacy within the monastic tradition holds lessons and models that single Christians today could benefit from. Unfortunately, Foster did not do this, resulting in contradictions of what was meant by the monastic vow of celibacy.

3. Richard Foster, *Money, Sex, and Power* (San Francisco: Harper & Row, 1985) 128–29.

4. Thomas Jones, *Sex and Love: When You're Single Again* (Nashville: Nelson, 1990), 162–63; see also p. 158.

5. Lewis Smedes, *Sex for Christians*, 152.

Chapter 10: Should Singles Feel Compelled to Be Sexually Intimate?

1. Richard Foster, *Money, Sex, and Power*, 130.

2. Ibid.

3. Ibid., 7–8

4. Walter Trobisch, *I Married You*, 79–80.

Chapter 12: What About Living Together Before Marriage?

1. John Shelby Sprong, *Living in Sin?: A Bishop Rethinks Human Sexuality* (San Francisco: Harper/Collins, 1988), 177.

2. Ibid., 178.

Chapter 14: Incompatability, Attractiveness, and Single Parenting

1. For more study on the topic of what sin is unforgiveable, read Mark 3:23–30 and Matthew 12:30–32.

2. Quoted in Dick Purnell, *Becoming a Friend and Lover* (San Bernardino, Calif.: Here's Life, 1986), 63.

3. Eugene Diamond and Rosemary Diamond, *The Positive Values of Chastity* (Chicago: Franciscan Herald, 1983), 2–3.

4. Gerhard Kittle, *Theological Dictionary of the New Testament*, vol. 6, (Grand Rapids: Eerdmans, 1968), 580–95.

Chapter 15: Masturbation, Fantasies, and Lust

1. As cited in Foster, *Money, Sex, and Power*, 123–124.

2. Harold Ivan Smith, "Dealing with the Question of Masturbation," speech to the National Association of Single Adult Leaders Consortium, San Francisco, 12 May 1992.

3. This historical survey is based on Uta Ranke-Heinemann, *Eunuchs for the Kingdom of Heaven* (New York: Doubleday, 1990), 311–30.

4. Cited in Ranke-Heinemann, *Eunuchs for the Kingdom of God,* 313. Bekker's book, *Onania or the Loathsome Sin of Self-Pollution,* was published in 1710.

5. Donald Goergen, *The Sexual Celibate* (New York: Seabury, 1974), 202–3.

6. Frederick Beuchner, *Godric* (San Francisco, Harper and Row, 1980), 153.

7. Lewis Smedes, *Sex for Christians,* 210.

8. "The War Within: An Anatomy of Lust," *Leadership Journal,* Fall 1982, 43.

Moody Press, a ministry of the Moody Bible Institute,
is designed for education, evangelization, and edification.
If we may assist you in knowing more about Christ
and the Christian life, please write us without obligation:
Moody Press, c/o MLM, Chicago, Illinois 60610.